POCKET EDITION

CONVERSATIONS

with

CREATIVE WOMEN

{ VOLUME ONE }

T0362671

Interviews about the careers and creative lives of 15 Australian women

by Tess McCabe

Conversations with Creative Women was first published in 2011.

Pocket Edition published 2019 by Creative Minds — creativemindshq.com

A catalogue record for this book is available from the National Library of Australia at catalogue.nla.gov.au

Design by Tess McCabe — tessmccabe.com.au

ISBN 9780994627322

You can't use up creativity. The more you use, the more you have.

Maya Angelou

CONTENTS

The idea to put together this book first popped into my brain in early 2011. I'm always coming up with ideas—for craft projects, for events, for websites, for businesses... it's surely a common thing amongst creative people and I definitely don't act on each and every one of them.

I often think that feeling empowered to emulate the success of a creative businesswoman is one thing, but feeling a sense of deflation that one's career goals have not yet been achieved is an all-too-common affliction. Everyone has their moments of self-doubt, and I am always interested in learning how different creatives overcome these and other issues relating to creative inspiration and running a profitable business or maintaining a fulfilling career.

There is no doubt that being a woman also presents its own unique career challenges, whether it be forging a path in a niche or male-dominated industry, or sustaining a fulfilling work life whilst caring for children and family. It's my hope that this book offers some insight into these topics and opens up discussion as to how we can all work smarter, not harder, in our creative lives.

I feel humbled and honoured that all the women I approached to be interviewed for this book enthusiastically agreed, despite my not having met many of them personally. They are at various stages of their careers, with varying responsibilities at home, as an employee, as a self-employed freelancer or as a business owner. Each and every one answered my questions with insight and generosity.

I hope *Conversations with Creative Women* will be a reference guide for you, your friends, and the other creative women in your life, or at the very least, an enjoyable 'sneak peek' into the lives of fifteen creative women.

I would encourage anyone with a passion for design to start small, and enjoy the process. If you love what you do, it will show in your work and other people will appreciate that.

KRISTEN DORAN

Textile designer

Kristen Doran Design is the home-based textile business of Kristen Doran, selling to stores around Australia and the world. All the fabrics are screen printed in Sydney, Australia and feature original designs ready for sewing.

Kristen's customers create cushions, bags, toys and clothing from her fabrics, making a stand against mass-production and enjoying the satisfaction of handmade. The all-natural basecloths (organic cotton, hemp/organic cotton and linen) used to print her designs are sourced from around the world and produced ethically.

Tell us about your early career beginnings… Do you have a tertiary background in textile design?

I studied fashion design at TAFE in East Sydney from 1988–1990 and loved every minute.

But it quickly (and I'd have to say painfully) became clear that this wasn't a perfect fit for me. I loved drawing, screen printing and sewing. But designing garments that were the cutting edge of fashion did not come easily. I did finish the three-year course and went to work in the fashion industry for six years—first in retail and then in manufacturing as a fashion illustrator and textile designer.

I went back to study graphic design at TAFE four nights a week while working full-time. And that is where I found my passion. I then went on to work in the communications department of a church-based charity for two-and-a-half years until I left to travel overseas for a year.

Kristen Doran Design started in a very small way back in 2002 with the drive to do something creative after the birth of my first child. I designed and sewed handbags and soft toys for family and friends using a mix of vintage fabrics and trims. Once that stash of goodies ran out I started researching hand screen printed fabrics in Australia—something to make my bags stand out in the crowd.

In 2005 I dragged out my old silk screen from college days and printed a few pieces of fabric on my back deck. I then sold these designs to a local art gallery. The thrill of seeing people like and actually buy my work spurred me on to find a printer to do the dirty work!

When did you start to feel like you could make a business out of designing and making your own line of products and textiles?

I blame it on the Internet! In 2005 I stumbled across a craft blog. Joy. A whole world of other crafty people out there documenting their daily lives with the same passion for craft that I had. I started my own blog six months later, sharing photos of bags and toys made from my own textile designs. Other bloggers from around the world started to ask where they could buy the fabric. A light bulb moment had me realise that selling the fabrics was so much easier than producing bags and by this time I had two little kids needing my time and attention.

My screen printer runs his own business locally and with his great technical knowledge I have been able to develop and grow my range of fabrics into something I'm very passionate about. Local and interstate craft stores that have contacted me to stock my fabrics have also been a great support and helped me realise that this was something I could do full-time to support my family.

How did you find a screen printer to produce your textiles? How has that relationship developed as your business has grown?

My printer is an old friend. But he didn't specialise in water-based inks, so it was a steep learning curve for him and his employees. I have to say it took about two years until I was totally happy about the quality of what we were producing together. He is fantastic to work with and even on his grumpy days I can still nag him to get my work done before other clients… well, sometimes. He also travels a fair bit looking into new technology in the industry and sharing his information with me. The company has just bought a small digital fabric printer, so I might get to play around with that and come up with some new concepts.

What is your process for designing your fabrics — do you draw a design by hand first? How long does a new design take to go from an idea to a printed bolt of fabric?

When it comes to my creativity I'd have to say there is no set formula. I can be a bit all over the place. Mostly I will hand draw a few concepts and then scan them into the computer to rework. Or sometimes I will use a photograph I have taken and turn this into an illustration. Lots of playing around for hours, sticking up printouts around the house to consider the scale and balance and even asking my two sons what they think.

I'd have to say my favourite way to create a print is hand sketching. After sketching all the elements needed for a design, I will then scan it into the computer, clean up the files and then the fun begins. Rearranging, colouring and generally playing with the design until I have the 'ahhh' moment and know to stop.

You have an impressive list of stockists as well as your own online shop. How much an average week is coordinating orders for retailers and direct customers? Do you have any specific systems in place to ensure this side of your business runs smoothly?

Most of the week is spent dealing with stockists. Only a tiny percentage is working on my online store. This wasn't always the way. When I first started up nearly all my sales were direct to my retail customers. But as time has passed new online fabrics stores have arrived on the scene and I deal with them mostly. I still keep my online store running, but it's usually stocked with the end of runs I have had printed up for wholesale customers.

Do you set yourself any limits (or targets) on how many stockists carry the Kristen Doran range?

Stockists contact me via my blog and shop and I send them wholesale prices. This has been a very natural process and has allowed me to grow my business at a slow and steady rate that suits my family lifestyle. I plan to be more proactive in this process this year.

Has there ever been a time when you felt you had taken too much on, or that your business wasn't in a place you wanted it to be? How did you manage that situation?

Every now and again I second guess myself. Wonder what on earth I am doing and think that no one will like/buy my designs. It's usually at this point a lovely customer will send me an email out of the blue with encouraging words that I truly appreciate and keep me going. I keep all of these in a file just in case the doubts creep in again and I need a boost. It's a little tricky working alone. There's no one around to give you feedback to know if you are still on track.

Did anything surprise you about making what you love doing into your full-time work?

Yes, that it's actually possible! I'm thankful everyday, even the boring ones where all I do is invoice and pack fabrics for posting. I have worked in offices for other people and while it's great to come home and be able to switch off for the night, I find working for myself with all the extra worries so much more fulfilling. The opportunity to walk my boys to school every morning is also another blessing.

I would encourage anyone with a passion for design to start small, and enjoy the process. If you love what you do, it will show in your work and other people will appreciate that.

Do you supplement the income you gain from your own range with any other work?

Yes, I do freelance graphic design for a few clients creating logos, brochures, DVD covers and book layouts. It's great to take a break from fabrics and focus on something different for a while. It keeps me fresh and my computer skills current. I'd say my time split 70% textiles and 30% graphic design. But when I first started selling fabrics the percentages were reversed. I'm very happy with the balance of work now and hope it continues this way.

Have there been any products or designs that you yourself love, but didn't sell as well as you expected, or vice versa?

Sure have! There is one design that customers just can't get enough of and it surprises me to this day. Don't get me wrong, I love it too… it's just the demand for this print is way more than all the others. It's currently available as a craft panel, but I have a stockist nagging me to turn it into a yardage print and I'm pretty sure that's a good idea. So when I have a spare day to sit and work on the computer, that's the plan.

Do you set yourself benchmarks or targets to work towards, or have a plan or roadmap in your own business?

I have a rough idea of how many new designs I would like to produce, how many markets to attend in a year and what type of products I'd like to focus on. The amount of new designs produced is more of a financial decision as there is a fair investment up front (paying for film, screens and sample prints). The amount of markets I do is a family decision, based on how long the markets run for and if they are interstate.

Are there other creative or textile design businesses that you see as inspirational, or at a place that you aspire to be?

I love Cloth Fabrics, Surface Art, Prints Charming, Bird Textiles and Ink & Spindle. All great Australian textile designers.

How do you maintain a balance between family life and the various tasks associated with running your own business?

When my kids were little, I used to work at night. That was very tiring, but at the same time I drew energy from being creative.

Now they are both at school I am able to work during the day and save nighttime for sleeping.

After so many years, what is it that continues to excite or energise you about running your own business?

I love being creative. I couldn't imagine doing anything else. This thought energises me to run my own business. To be in charge of my own days is something I appreciate and don't take for granted.

Where would you like Kristen Doran Design to be in five or 10 years time?

I would love a store/work space not in my home! A place to run workshops and share my experience with other crafters would be fantastic. And a few employees to take over the mundane tasks would be nice too.

....

When you first start writing a blog there is literally nobody reading, which is a good thing whilst you find your 'voice'. As soon as you see some traction and some solid readership, I guess it does help keep you 'on mission'.

....

LUCY FEAGINS

Blogger and stylist

Lucy Feagins is a Melbourne-based stylist,
writer and design blogger. Her blog, The Design Files,
launched in early 2008 and attracts a readership of over
400,000 page views a month from around the globe.

The Design Files has been featured in publications
including *The Age*, *The Good Weekend, Urbis, Design Quarterly*, *Inside
Out Magazine* and *Real Living Magazine*. In 2009 it was named by
The Times (UK) as one of the world's Top 50 design blogs.

Lucy has contributed to various Australian design
and lifestyle publications including *The Age Melbourne
Magazine*, *Inside Out*, *Design Quarterly* and *Artichoke Magazine*.

When you left school, what did you study at university? Did you have a clear idea of the kind of career you wanted?

I didn't have much idea what I wanted to be at all when I finished school, actually. I went to a great high school and did quite well at school generally, but there was a real focus on academic achievement at my school, and the idea of doing something creative or a bit left of centre didn't really enter my brain whilst at high school. I figured I'd do a creative university course and work it out from there!

I took a course called 'Bachelor of Creative Arts' which was a strange but fantastic hybrid Melbourne University/Victorian College of the Arts course. It doesn't exist anymore, sadly. It was very broad and gave me the opportunity to study fine art, film making, art history and film theory all in one degree. I ended up doing Honours and majoring in film... Which led to me working in film when I first finished university.

You spent many years in the film and television industry working in set design and styling... What types of projects did you work on? And what did your day-to-day entail?

I worked in the film industry from when I left uni until late last year—2003 to 2010. When you study film, most people you meet at uni want to direct, but I was always keen on working in the set design department.

When I finished university I got a few months of unpaid work experience at a couple of Melbourne production companies (mainly working on TV commercials). I met a few production designers and ended up assisting them on a freelance basis for not very much money! I just drove around Melbourne running errands and sourcing props and collecting things and returning things, and hung out on set mainly on TV commercials (TVCs). I met a lovely lady who became a bit of a mentor for me—Suki Ibbetson. She employed me off and on for about four years. It was a great intro into the industry but was also very unreliable work—I held onto a retail job for the first few years. Eventually I moved away from TVCs and into TV series, and made enough contacts to keep myself almost solidly employed as a set dresser.

In Melbourne there isn't a whole lot of variety when it comes to film projects—you kind of take whatever is on offer! I ended up doing lots of commercials, quite a lot of kids' TV shows (The Elephant Princess and Dead Gorgeous—I don't expect anyone over age 13 has ever heard of them!) and lots of comedy—one of my biggest contracts was working on Thank God You're Here (TGYH) over four series. It was a huge success so that kept me busy for a few years. It was a huge effort, very cheesy, very varied, and lots of fun but very exhausting!

The last thing I worked on was a feature film from Working Dog, the same production company as TGYH. It's working title is '25' but that is likely to change. I am not sure when it'll hit cinemas—maybe next year?

I finished working in film at the end of 2010 because it all got a bit much as The Design Files has snowballed out of control! A standard week in the film industry is 50 hours—and that often turns into overtime and super early starts/late finishes etc when you're shooting. It's a hard job to do when you have an equally demanding side project!

You started The Design Files (TDF) in January 2008—was starting a blog a New Year's resolution?

You know what, Tess, I can't remember! I think probably yes! I have flirted on and off with the idea of writing 'goals' at the start of every year. I don't know if it's working because I don't think I ever remember where they are to crosscheck after the year is up!

Your blog readership grew substantially after a post about a local Melbourne artist was referenced on the popular American design blog, Design*Sponge. Did you feel any pressure knowing that so many more people were now reading your posts?

Yes, I guess that particular example was a turning point which motivated me to write regularly and keep the content interesting and original. When you first start writing a blog there is literally nobody reading, which is a good thing whilst you find your 'voice'. As soon as you see some traction and some solid readership I guess it does help keep you 'on mission'.

In general though, I really don't think too much about how many people are tuning in to read TDF everyday. I am SO grateful for the immense support and readership The Design Files has, but I think it would be a bit paralysing if I had every reader in mind whenever I'm churning out a post. I would be way too self-conscious and it probably would end up far too edited. Instead I try to write quickly, in the same way that I speak, and not edit too much.

When did you decide to leave the film & TV industry and commit to blogging full-time?

End of 2010. I worked on what was basically my 'dream job'—as assistant art director on a Melbourne-made feature film. It was a great job and would have made me really happy earlier in my career... But working on this film made me realise how tricky it was getting to juggle TDF with full-time work, and in the end I guess it was the final push I needed to take the leap into full-time blogging!

Did you develop a long-term plan for your business when you decided that The Design Files would become your main source of income?

No. I am shocking with things like that. I did do some cash flow projections and budgeting and goal setting stuff—but not a strict business plan. I don't even know what one looks like.

In general terms I find separating work and life pretty much impossible—so rather than build a 'business plan' I seem to just generate general 'life plans'! Does that count?!

How has your work routine changed now that you only work on the blog? Do you keep to a Monday-Friday workweek or is TDF a 24/7 business?

TDF is pretty all-consuming to be honest. I certainly work beyond normal business hours. I work late into the night most weeknights and I can't avoid working on Sundays because there's always content to upload and sort through for the start of the week.

Also I can't figure out how to take an overseas holiday without checking in to the web each day—even if posts are scheduled whilst I am gone, there are always endless emails, advertising enquiries, submissions and comment moderation etc.

Having said that, it is AWESOME being my own boss and I wouldn't change that for anything. It means I can be flexible. If I have a really late night (which often happens!), I can sleep in a bit the next day. I am a bit of a workaholic but I don't know any independent creative person who isn't.

Unlike some professional bloggers, you curate all your advertising and don't engage a third party for help. How much of your time is spent finding and managing The Design Files' advertisers?

I spend no time finding advertisers, but I spend a lot of time managing them!

TDF had gained a really strong readership before I began offering advertising, and because I wasn't reliant on it as my source of income until relatively recently, I wasn't fussed about approaching or seeking out advertising. As with most decisions I have made so far with the blog, I allowed this to develop organically, and I'm lucky that I've never been short of advertising requests.

Managing advertisers is something that is quite labour-intensive but I feel it's worth it, to ensure ads on the site are relevant to the content, attractive and not annoying! The click rate for most ads on my site is far above the standard average for web advertising—and that's because the ads are not ugly or intrusive.

I do find a massive chunk of my week these days is about managing ad bookings and advertiser requests... It's not super fun, but to be honest I feel that having a good relationship with the advertisers is really important, and can't be separated from my role as editor of the site. Looking after advertisers is as much my job these days as generating content is. I would say I probably spend two-thirds of my time generating content and one-third dealing with advertising.

Have you been offered any professional opportunities due to the popularity of your blog that have surprised you?

Yes, I've been offered a few opportunities to promote completely random products (such as alcohol and ice cream brands!) for next to no money! This is a real trend with marketing companies at the moment. I get the impression that bloggers are seen as some kind of resource who will do anything for very little remuneration. I figure if you're paying a marketing company to dream up a social media campaign for you, you can probably afford to pay a high profile blogger fairly to assist promoting it!

On a more positive note, I have been offered a few publishing deals, which is pretty awesome. I have yet to take up this offer though—no time!

While many in the Australian design community know The Design Files, and are aware of the status of popular design blogs, have you come across people who don't understand the industry at all? How has this affected your business?

When I first started writing the blog in 2008 you'd be surprised how many people had not heard of the word 'blog'. Boy how that has changed! These days every creative company seems to have one.

These days I rarely come across someone who isn't across the whole design blogging thing. It is actually very rare... like... nonexistent. I do come across people who have never seen my blog specifically, but generally most people are vaguely across the general phenomenon, and are usually inquisitive/interested!

The Design Files now features a weekly home tour and a weekly interview with someone in the art and design community — how far in advance do you plan these features? Have there ever been instances where a feature has fallen through at the last minute?

I plan the home tours about three to four weeks in advance, and the interviews anywhere from two to six weeks in advance. I try to keep it under four weeks though, because a) it's easier to write about whilst it's fresh in my mind, and b) sometimes the longer the lead time, the slower the response!

I am quite often in a position where something falls through at the last minute. Sometimes Guest Bloggers flake out on us a week or so out too. When that happens I just wrack my brains and beg someone to do it and usually thank GOD they agree. Jenny (Butler, my sub-editor) is always very impressed when I pull some magic out of the hat at the last minute. It's a little easier now TDF has a bit of pull!

A popular blog often draws a lot of comments, but not all of them are positive. How do you deal with negative comments and how does it affect you as the author of the post?

I shouldn't take it personally, but on the rare occasion that TDF receives a negative comment, I do get a bit hurt/annoyed! Mainly because it's usually directed at the product/design/home I'm featuring, not me personally, hence I feel an obligation to protect whoever's work is up for discussion.

Frankly I am getting a bit grumpier after being four years in the blogging business(!) but I figure everyone gets to read TDF for FREE, it's not like you've paid money to buy a magazine. If you're not massively in love with something we post on any given day—chill out! It's not the end of the world. Sometimes I just want to write 'would you like a refund!' Too harsh?

If a particular comment really bugs me these days, I don't have any qualms about deleting it. At the end of the day, TDF is my creation and I want to keep it a happy and constructive place!

Who do you admire in the online/offline community?

SO many! I admire Jeremy Wortsman at the Jacky Winter Group—he's created a brilliant business from virtually nothing and is always pushing the boundaries.

I admire Grace Bonney, editor of Design*Sponge in the US—a true pioneer in the design blogging community, and endlessly generous with her wisdom and advice.

I admire my friend Megan Morton who is an interiors stylist in Sydney. Her business has so may facets—she has grown her brand well beyond the traditional limits of freelance styling. She's also a busy hands-on mum to three kids, and she's another incredible example of someone who is truly generous with their wisdom and advice.

I admire Beci Orpin—an incredibly talented illustrator and designer, another hard working hands-on mum... someone who says yes to pretty much anything you can throw at her and never complains about being too busy or having two kids to look after! Working mums in general are my heroes.

I admire Kon Karapanagiotidis who is the CEO and founder of the Asylum Seeker Resource Centre in Melbourne. He is a brilliant man and the ASRC is an incredible independent initiative.

What is the biggest misconception about the life of a full-time design blogger?
That I know anything about social media!

A craftsperson must have a fundamental desire to make things, to refine and practice techniques and not be afraid to fail the first time.

MARIAN HOSKING

Jeweller and silversmith

Dr Marian Hosking is an educator, jeweller and silversmith. She regularly exhibits her work in Australia, Europe and the Asia Pacific region. Currently a Senior Lecturer at Monash University and Coordinator of the Metals and Jewellery Studio within the Faculty of Art, Design and Architecture, she has been an educator in her field for over 30 years.

With the benefit of intensive practice she has developed a personal vocabulary in her work to express a specific vision and interpretation of the qualities of Australian light and landscape. Marian favours the soft white sheen of silver, with its evasive highlights and shifting shadows.

She has work in the collections of most Australian state art galleries, including the National Gallery of Australia and the Art Gallery of Aberdeen. Marian is represented in Australia by Gallery Funaki, Melbourne, and Bilk, Canberra, in Europe by Galerie Ra, Amsterdam and in the United States by Charon Kransen Fine Arts.

Your career as a jeweller and artist has spanned an impressive four decades... Can you tell us a bit about your creative path over that time? Have you taken breaks or worked in other mediums or industries?

I studied gold and silversmithing at RMIT University straight after completing high school. I had received a scholarship to study Architecture at Melbourne University, but quickly transferred to gold and silversmithing at RMIT, a decision I have been very happy with.

I have practiced as a jeweller and silversmith continuously since graduating, the main gaps being on the birth of my two children. I am also an educator in the field of jewellery and metalsmithing.

How has your aesthetic as a jeweller evolved or matured throughout your career?

Life impacts on the direction of my practice, however some things remain fundamental. I enjoy silver as a medium and still find it has challenges and qualities to keep me working with it. The natural environment is a constant source of inspiration and reflection for me.

You have studied and spent time overseas throughout your creative life — given that natural forms in flora and fauna is a recurring theme in your work, how did these new environments affect you creatively?

Studying in Pforzheim, Germany, in the early 1970s altered the emphasis in my work from making with a design emphasis to a more personal and unlimited approach. Returning to Australia after two years in Germany emphasised my commitment to the Australian environment. Travel and studying overseas are educationally stimulating. I do work with plants I encounter both here and in my travels, but predominantly I am interested in issues that I have first-hand knowledge of, and that is mostly Australia.

Do you have a workshop at home, or a studio set-up elsewhere?

I have always maintained a workshop in my own home, and for three years I shared in Workshop 3000 (based in Melbourne).

What is your process for starting a new work? How much research, sketching, drawing and planning is done before you begin working with silver?

I am constantly thinking, reading, observing and exploring what and how I shall make the next piece. I take photographs, draw, collect samples, read and discuss. Observation and selection and the filtering of a motif or idea is ongoing. I do not make models prior to making but I do experiment and refine techniques and materials. Of course, I have a backlog of information accumulating but am also constantly learning.

Do you conceive of your jewellery designs in terms of collections, or one-off pieces?

My working process is quite evolutionary—one piece leads to another, sometimes they form groups, and sometimes they are on their own—but mostly one piece influences another or reflects an idea from somewhere else.

Your work has been displayed in numerous exhibitions in Australia and overseas and you have been the recipient of multiple awards—how much of your time is spent researching these opportunities and coordinating work to be sent to galleries and exhibitions?

I am constantly thinking ahead, but also opportunities are often being thrust at me, deciding which way to go and which exhibition to follow through on is a constant aspect of making. Keeping a good photographic record of work is essential and applying for projects that are of particular interest. Not all proposals are successful but you must keep pursuing a goal, despite knockbacks.

Have you applied for grants or funding at any stage of your career?

I have been very fortunate in receiving funding from the Australia Council for the Arts, Arts Victoria and Monash University. I do apply for funding and am not always successful.

Do you consciously differentiate between making products for a gallery environment and products for sale?

I only make for exhibitions, competitions and specialist jewellery galleries. When I started there were no specialist venues, but I did have exhibitions and had work in a few craft outlets. I find the paperwork associated with keeping track of work on consignment a waste of my time, so I prefer to deal only with a few galleries.

You've been heavily involved in the Australian craft scene for many years — in your opinion, how has the view of crafts people changed in the public's eye over that time? And do you see different attitudes toward craft practices within different generations?

I am proud to be a craft practitioner and even an artisan, as making is an essential aspect of my practice. I value craft in many forms, functional crafts and especially jewellery, which I consider has an emotional function. In the 1970s craft was perhaps a lifestyle choice by some but not by me—there are as many attitudes to crafting and its appreciation as there are craft workers. It is not for me to comment on generational change.

Can you tell us about your PhD, Crafting and meaning: Allusion, motif and identity in Australian jewellery and small-scale silver objects: a studio-based exploration — what did you set out to discover through your research?

My research undertaken toward a PhD enabled me to better position myself in the creative field. I explored historic and contemporary texts and improved my writing skills.

What skills do you think are essential for someone looking to forge a fulfilling career in a craft practice?

A craft person must have a fundamental desire to make things, to refine and practice techniques and not be afraid to fail the first time. To explore and be open to the challenges and discoveries along the way. Persistence is required in any field to achieve a sustaining career.

I learned early on that the time and effort you can spend on the 'next big thing', is better spent on attracting fewer but higher quality targeted visitors (to your website).

CLARE LANCASTER

Online consultant and blogger

Clare Lancaster graduated from a communication design degree in Brisbane in 2001 and accidently found herself working in a full-time job marketing websites on the Internet. This was okay because she had wanted to work online and always dreamed of running a business where she could travel and work regardless of where she was based.

She spent the next seven years working online, learning and observing. One day, she took the leap and started her own business. Clare soon found herself writing for magazines, doing work she loved and woke up one day to find her website womeninbusiness.com.au had been listed on Forbes.com (one of the world's leading business and technology websites). It was just as good as being featured on Etsy.com!

Clare has realised her dream of living and working from anywhere in the world, and is currently based in London planning the next chapter of her adventure.
She's never looked back.

You studied one of the first university degrees in Australia devoted to communication design in new media in 1998. Did you have a vision of what you wanted your career to focus on back then? And did you always know you'd start your own business at some point?

I think so, yes. From the moment we got dial-up Internet at home in 1996 I was hooked and knew that I wanted my career to be involved with the Internet in some way. I had always loved creating, exploring and was a bookworm, so being able to visit other countries virtually and discovering the abundance of information at my fingertips was like heaven to me.

When it came to deciding what to study after high school, my art teacher suggested the new communication design degree at Queensland University of Technology. I put a portfolio together and was accepted.

The degree was very hands-on which suited me perfectly and early on I could see working online was a great path to a flexible career. I come from an entrepreneurial-minded family and from when I was small, I was always coming up with little business ideas, from charging to perform magic tricks to running poker tournaments during maths class (that didn't end well). Running my own business was something I always wanted to do.

Why did you decide to focus your services on women in business, rather than, for example, creative businesses or micro/small businesses?

I'd started writing about other women doing business online on my personal blog when I was offered the opportunity to buy womeninbusiness.com.au. I think the phrase 'women in business' carries some outdated ideas with it. Many people think of women climbing corporate ladders or that cliché of red lipstick, stilettos and power suits. I think of something different—women who start businesses that combine the skills and experience they've collected with their passions to create something that matters to them. I see so many women turning to the Internet as a platform for their business and I wanted to use the experience that I had gained to help them navigate the online world and all that goes with it.

Can you explain how online marketing differs from other types of marketing?

I think the biggest difference is that it's a one-on-one conversation rather than a form of mass communication. The things I like most about it are that it's cheap (although more time consuming), targeted, and ideal for small business owners, especially women. Much of marketing online is media-based, creating and publishing content and with the rise of social media, networking in a very human and casual way.

The online world moves at a fast pace. In your 10 years experience you must have seen all kinds of Internet marketing fads come and go. How do you keep up with what is new in the social media and the online marketing world, and how do you distinguish successful online marketing avenues from the short-term fads?

The online world does move very fast. Websites have evolved from online brochures, to encouraging interactivity and now with blogging, they are almost a media asset for a business as well as a sales platform. User behaviours and expectations change quickly too and with the popularity of social networking platforms like Facebook, business owners now need to go away from their websites and spend time where their audience is to be noticed.

I learned early on that the time and effort you can spend on the next big thing is better spent on attracting fewer but higher-quality targeted visitors, giving them what they want on your website and keeping in touch with them in a way that's useful for everyone involved.

I rely on Twitter to filter my news and industry trends and am always experimenting with new things on my own websites.

Your blog is a mix of business advice, design finds and personal posts. Is it important to you that your personality is infused with the products you offer as a marketing professional? And is this a method that you find attracts your ideal client?

Absolutely. I think it's important for anyone doing business online to show their personality – one of the great things about doing business online is that it can be personal. One person working from home can develop a highly engaged audience that sustains their business. People are attracted to enthusiasm and personal stories; I'm very clear about who I want to help and who my products are designed for and use my blog posts to illustrate that and attract people who connect with what I'm saying.

Running an online business, what is a typical day for you?

In the beginning I resisted the idea of creating a typical day but now I know I need some structure to get the most out of my days. I start by checking my emails on my phone first thing when I wake up (a habit I'm trying to break). I read my favourite blogs with a cup of coffee and promote the day's blog post on Twitter and my Facebook page. Then I'll reply to emails, check the to-do list that I made the night before and start on my most important tasks.

I like to get out for fresh air during the day so I'll take my bike for a ride and visit my husband who works close by or take the train to one of London's beautiful parks or homeware stores and get things for dinner on the way back. When I get home I'll work on some more tasks, check my sales figures, write my to-do list for tomorrow, cook dinner, tidy up, then watch TV (usually with my laptop) or read before it's time to sleep.

What do you do to network and promote the products that you offer?

My blog and sending regular emails to my mailing list are my main marketing activities, followed closely by spending time on Twitter and on my Facebook page. I also spend time getting to know other bloggers with similar audiences to mine. 99% of my marketing and networking is done online.

You have recently made the move from Brisbane, Australia, to London, England. What systems or processes did you put in place to ensure your business is location-independent?

It was always my intention to create a location-independent business, so I had that in mind when I went from one-on-one consulting to creating products. The payment process and delivery of my products is 100% automated and happens entirely online.

You mention on your website that you do not want to scale your business up or take on staff... is this a long-term strategy? What methods are you employing to ensure your business can grow in revenue while remaining autonomous?

If there's one thing I've learned so far it's never say never, but right now I'm enjoying doing my own thing as a one-woman business. I like the flexibility and pace of keeping things small. For me scaling my business means creating more products to add to my range, marketing my online workshops and creating more workshops for my audience—something I can do from wherever I am in the world.

Who do you admire in the online business world?

I admire people who innovate and stay true to their vision. Bloggers like Holly Becker from Decor8blog.com and

Victoria Smith from SFGirlbyBay.com as well as bigger companies like Zappos and Net-a-porter. I have to mention local talent like Kate McKibbin from DropDeadGorgeous Daily.com and Naomi Simson, the founder of Red Balloon, a pioneer in online business in Australia.

What do you see as the unique challenges that women face in their own businesses or careers?

While I am as yet unqualified to comment, the obvious one is the challenge of being a mother and balancing fulfilling work with the reality of paying the bills. That aside, I think a big challenge is taking a chance and persisting with your big idea against pressure to take the obvious path from well meaning family and friends.

What has surprised you about the way your business has developed?

As my business has developed it's given me the confidence to work on what I'm most passionate about. At first I thought I needed to consult—it was the obvious path to help others one-on-one by sharing what I knew about online business. After a while I looked at that business model and decided that creating products based on what I knew would be easier to scale and allow me to reach more people. Now I'm in the process of creating a spin-off brand based on a poster I created for womeninbusiness.com.au that embraces my love of travel and encouraging people to act on their big ideas.

What are some of the lessons you have learned as a woman running an independent business?

The biggest one would be that you've got to believe in yourself and your potential and capabilities. For something that sounds 'up in the air', it's critical to your daily productivity and long-term performance! Another would be to take action when inspiration hits and don't wait until everything is perfect to go to market. I remember reading that Kristina Karlsson, who founded (paper goods label) Kikki-K, launched her business with one white box. It's better to have something out there that you can tweak based on feedback than to wait until things are perfect—you'll make changes anyway (and you should) and your business will develop as you go along. That's the beauty of independent business.

....

There's nothing wrong or uncool or unpretty about being a good and nice person. In fact, it'll take you a LONG way.

....

MARYANN TALIA PAU

Artist, weaver and designer

Born in Apia, Samoa, Maryann Talia Pau grew up in
Auckland, New Zealand, and then Melbourne, Australia.
Her work begins with Mana Couture body adornment, a
collection of Pacific couture and art using materials and
craft techniques from Samoa and across the Pacific.
Her other passions include siapo (Samoan bark cloth),
textiles and architecture. The heart of her practise is love
and mana, especially for the people and the beautiful
material culture of the Pacific. She also draws strength from
qualities such as courage, grace and generosity.

Maryann's first public exhibition was in August 2009 at
Craft Victoria. She then went on to exhibit in Sydney at
Object and Blacktown Arts Centre. This work led to her
debut solo exhibition, Fashioning the Mana, in February
2010 at the Oceanic Gallery, now known as Art of the
Pacific, at the National Gallery of Victoria. Three of
Maryann's breastplates are on display in the new Art of the
Pacific Gallery, NGV International, Melbourne Australia.

Maryann is a co-founder of the Pacific Women's Weaving
Circle and the Australian Pacific Arts Network. Maryann
is also a Chief of Haus of Savvy Savage with Chief Lia
Pa'apa'a, a new creative enterprise that showcases Pacific and
Indigenous art, design, lifestyles and collaborations.

Were you artistic from a young age? And when did you decide that you wanted to pursue a life as an artist and maker?

I was one of those kids that loved to make stuff out of anything, usually to fill time and because I was curious about materials. I was always trying to work out what I could play with, how could I manipulate materials to do what I wanted. I learnt how to listen and see when the material was trying to teach me something. Free play and experimenting has had a huge impact on how I approach my work. I don't ever want to lose my sense of playfulness and fun, I'm serious about my work, but I also embrace my craft with fearlessness and the belief that it will come together when it's meant to.

I decided to launch out as an artist and maker because I believed in the place from which my work comes from: love and love for my culture and mobs. I knew that this was enough to make it special, and that what ever I put my hand to, it would always be beautiful. My mum would always say to me, "Beautiful people, make beautiful things". And she wasn't talking about physical beauty. It's one of the best lessons my mama taught me. It's always been more than weaving, colour combinations and materials. My work talks about and calls on the creativity of my ancestors and I give it a fresh twist that makes sense to my urban reality in Australia. I am a maker and weaver, and I value the handmade, reusing, story telling and relationships.

What is 'Mana'? And how is it represented in your work?

Mana is a Samoan word and it is also a word found in several Pacific Island communities. It means spiritual and ancestral power. I find Mana to be one of the most beautiful words across the Pacific. I chose this word for my jewellery label Mana Couture, because I felt my works were more than fashion or couture, it embodied a special quality best described in my language as Mana, a divine power that is not purely from me. It's why so many people respond with positivity and emotion when they see or wear my work. Each piece is made with love and care and respect and people can feel that. It's always such a gift to hear how people are moved when then put on a piece of Mana Couture.

Can you tell us about your design and making process — do you start with sketches or drawings, experiment with materials, or do you have a fully-formed idea in your head before you start making?

I have to say it's a mixture of both. Sometimes I'll delve straight into something and learn and grow with it. Other times, I have a clear idea of a pair of earrings or a breastplate and this might be activated by a colour or lava lava (sarong) fabric that I've seen or pulled out from my stash. Both processes are enriching for me. Sometimes, a special event will drive a making process as well—I may want to whip up a pendant for an opening or launch party. I sometimes sketch down shapes, usually because my head is so full of ideas, I don't want to lose them!!

Your exhibition Fashioning the Mana in April 2011 was the first contemporary adornment by a Pacific woman to be showcased in the Oceanic gallery, now known as the Art of the Pacific gallery, NGV International. This is an incredible achievement for an emerging artist — can you tell us a bit about how this opportunity came about?

It is quite amazing, and I can only put it down to timing and being blessed. I made contact with Sana Balai, who is the Assistant Curator for Indigenous Art (she is also affectionately known as Aunty). I wanted to introduce myself and ask to view a tapa covered denim outfit by another artist, Rosanna Raymond (who I adore) which the gallery purchased in 1997.

After a meeting with Aunty Sana and Judith Ryan, the Senior Curator for Indigenous Art, they soon came to see my work in Sydney, Precious Pendants at Object, and then we discussed the possibility of me showing work next to Rosanna's in the Oceanic gallery for L'Oreal Melbourne Fashion Festival's Cultural Program, March 2010.

I became the first Pacific Islander artist to have work purchased by the Foundation for Living Australian Artists and the first contemporary Polynesian artist to have work purchased for Art of the Pacific Collection which is currently exhibiting at NGV International. I am also the first woman with Pacific Islander heritage to have work shown in the original Oceanic gallery on ground floor at NGV, a space which normally exhibited works by men only.

A desire to reach out and connect with other art works and a willingness to meet and chat led to this incredible opportunity. It's definitely a highlight in my career to date!

Tell us about the Pacific Women's Weaving Circle, the Melbourne-based group you co-founded. What made you decide to start the group and what does it hope to achieve?

The Pacific Women's Weaving Circle is new a collective that Lisa Hilli (media artist) and I established last year. It's a safe space for Pacific Islander women to come together to share and teach Pacific crafts like weaving. We meet once a month and we have a great weave jam, a great feed and a good laugh. It was another one of those conversations where we expressed a need and we made it happen with the support of friends and family.

This year, we welcomed Lia Pa'apa'a and Grace Vanilau to the management team and we are quickly becoming a well oiled and efficient team that oversees general running and admin tasks, grant applications, projects and collaborations

I decided to launch out as an artist and maker because I believed in the place from which my work comes from: love and love for my culture and mobs. I knew that this was enough to make it special.

and market opportunities for women to sell their beautiful Melbourne-made Pacific craft. It's a special space and I am very proud to be a part of it and to watch it grow and support other highly skilled weavers in our community.

Most of us in the circle live away from our extended families and parents, who would normally pass down these special crafts of weaving so we thought, why not create something like that but tap into local knowledge for support and community. I've had visions of being part of a circle of women who meet, have a gossip and laugh and maybe a little cry but would get some serious and deliciously beautiful weaving done in the same time. I figured if I loved weaving there would surely be others out there.

The spirit of the circle is warm and generous and uplifting and we recognise it has to be modeled by the management team. We've had some amazing collaborations along the way, with the South Project, Alwin Reamillio and Mis Design, a collaboration with Alphaville in Fitzroy for the Ian Potter Museum of Art, University of Melbourne. We are showing how weaving is a powerful tool for building peaceful and creative communities.

Can you explain a little about why craft and making is important to women in Samoa?

I realised a few years ago that my other passions, siapo (Samoan bark cloth) and ie toga (Samoan finely woven pandanus mats) are the works of women. It is the domain and creative expression of women that produces these beautiful textiles. Both siapo and ie toga are used as dress for special occasions and are highly valued items that are exchanged during ceremonies such as weddings or funerals. For many women, making and selling these provide a significant source of income for her and her family.

How often do you travel back to Samoa and New Zealand, and how do these experiences enhance your creative work?

As an adult I have returned to Samoa and New Zealand once, and both occasions were enough to confirm for me my desire to make and continue these old crafts. After my trip to Samoa in 2008, I returned to launch Mana Couture and registered it as a business name. The following year, I would make the transition to being a full-time artist and maker and apply to be in my first exhibition with my breast plate, "Fa'amolemole, pe mafai ona tatou lalaga fa'atasi?" Samoan for, "Please can I weave with you?" After my trip to Auckland this year in March, I returned with a new special tatau (tattoo) by a dear friend, and I felt ready to launch Haus of Savvy Savage, my latest adventure and long term enterprise project.

In Melbourne you have been involved in many projects with The Social Studio. How have the techniques of women from other cultures represented there affected your own work?

This collaboration was a powerful reminder of why I love weaving and how a universal craft such as this can be a beautiful language that many people can use to celebrate their identity. When I went in to The Social Studio late last year, some of the women recognised some of the weaving techniques and would bring along something that they made or was from their country or village. The resemblances were astounding, the shapes, the geometry and colours; and the stories of learning or watching as a child, even more so. I loved hearing how weaving could take some of them back to their childhood, and remind them of simple pleasures, like aunties being cheeky or laughing so loud it was scary!

Your own work beautifully combines traditional Pacific craft techniques with the drama and elaborate detailing of couture fashion. Do you see yourself branching into fashion design in the future, or would you like to collaborate with garment designers on a collection?

It's inevitable that I end up moving into fashion. Some of my breastplates are so big it could be worn on it's own! I've taken it as slow as possible but there are designs that are bursting to come out soon. They just need a bit more time to develop and then they'll be ready. Sometimes, it's simply a matter of just doing it and seeing what happens.

I'd love to produce a line of fashion clothing for Haus of Savvy Savage, through Mana Couture and with my co-Chief Lia Pa'apa'a. I love collaborations as well, it's just a matter of finding the best fit. There's so many great designers out there, and I'd love to strike a balance of designing our own and creating with someone else.

From your own art practice, to workshops, exhibitions, collaborations and creative side-businesses, you seem to always be undertaking many projects at once! How do you balance all your creative projects with raising a young family, and do you ever feel the need to take time out in order to reinvigorate your creativity?

All the time! This year has been extraordinary in that some of these projects were planted last year and are coming to fruition now, and others were great opportunities that came my way and were too good to say no. All of them though have a special something, which is attributed mainly to the quality and character of the person and project. Even in my sometimes overtired state, I can see the lessons I needed to learn quick smart, about myself and my practice, about others and about quality and integrity. I've got exceptional people around me. My husband is amazingly talented and supportive and we love our children and family dearly. I have a great network of sistas and friends, and mentors who I can have frank and safe conversations with. If I need a break, I try to take it and if I don't, I've got lots of people around me to tell me so!! A cup of tea and a manicure and pedicure goes a long way!!

What advice would you give to others who wish to reengage with their ancestry and culture or pass on their artistic skills to others?

It's important for people to know that ancestry and culture is never lost. It's always there lingering somewhere deep inside, it just needs some dedicated time and effort and it will reveal itself, often when you are truly ready. A lot of the time it's about owning who you are, and not trying to copy someone else or exoticise someone else and their culture. That's when people start copying and appropriating, which is not cool. Be your best, is what I always say, because only you can do that better than any one else.

Passing on knowledge and skills is crucial to my work, which is why the Pacific Women's Weaving Circle is so important to me. The skills I learn or have taught myself don't belong to me, they belong to my family and communities. What matters is how we use them to uplift our communities and families and be role models of generosity and light. It's a huge responsibility as well, I am answerable to my family and community. Some of us carry some special knowledge and not everyone can use it, it's why communities are so necessary—they help us navigate our way through and pull you into line when needed.

Can you offer any advice to emerging artists who are starting their careers on networking and creating opportunities for themselves?

Some tried and true lessons:
» Be bold and creative.
» Follow your gut feeling about a project or people.
» Surround yourself with the best people because you don't

know all the answers, they do. You know your craft and skill, just do that.

» Be humble. That doesn't mean you let people walk all over you or that you have to walk with your head down. It takes practice and you can even see humility and grace in people's walk. People don't mind a show-off but save it for when it really, really matters, otherwise you become predictable. There's nothing wrong or uncool or unpretty about being a good and nice person. In fact, it'll take you a LONG way. Save the attitude for when it really matters and always let your work speak for itself. If you have to talk too much about it for it to get noticed, there's something wrong.

» Love who you are and what you do, that always shines through and is ultimately what will attract the right people to you.

CRISTINA RE

Designer

Cristina Re is one of Australia's leading designers. Recognised for her elegant signature feminine style, Cristina aims to inspire and delight with her beautiful decorative patterns featured on a range of stationery, paper, fashion and lifestyle products.

Cristina's products are artistically beautiful and of the finest quality. She is committed to creating collections that tell a unique story and provide the ultimate sensory experience. Furthermore, she believes in the idea of offering luxury goods at an affordable price and available to all who love her brand.

Cristina is challenged to transform the ordinary into extraordinary and sees an opportunity everywhere to bring a little decoration and fabulousness to everyday objects (she blames it on her Italian heritage). Her philosophy is that "less is never more" and believes that it is a necessity to indulge in beautiful things that make you feel good, are fashion forward and that stimulate the senses. Cristina believes every day is an occasion to celebrate your creativity. Creativity does not just mean making a piece of art or handmade card, creativity to her means designing your life just the way you want to be, and living your bliss.

After studying photography as part of your Bachelor of Art, you started your own photography studio upon graduation. Can you tell us a bit about that time? What drew you to photography and working for yourself in that field?

After graduating at Swinburne University with an Honours degree in design and photography, I worked as a photographer's assistant for a wedding photography studio. After only a short period of time, I started my own business with a vision to offer brides a more feminine and fashionable approach to wedding photography. At the time, I was one of the only female photographers around, as the industry was very male dominated.

It seemed to me that part of my success was due to the fact that many women felt much more comfortable with a female photographer who seemed to understand their needs, and knew how to bring out the best in them on the day. I liked to make them feel like fashion models, understanding that every woman wants to be beautiful on her special day.

My main focus was to offer a unique experience, which encompassed offering everything from the photography, to customised wedding stationery and wedding albums with a designer touch. The response and demand for my invitation creations was overwhelming. It was then that I discovered a niche in the industry for beautiful and contemporary DIY stationery.

How did you then make the move into building the Cristina Re product range — was this something you always planned to do?

Whilst I was shooting weddings I started to design on the side with a vision to express my creativity and get my work 'out there' in the industry. I found that the stationery ranges available were very traditional at the time, so I started putting my pattern designs on cards and letter writing sets that people could purchase in specialty gift stores. I soon started receiving requests for A4-size papers that could be laser printable and customised into wedding invitations at home. This was how the DIY concept originated.

I had not planned to create a DIY stationery line, however I always wanted to have my own range of stationery.

What kinds of skills did you identify in yourself early on that made you realise you could take your artistic talents and build thriving businesses? Did you study business at any time?

I didn't study business and didn't have any real experience working in the industry. I pretty much started my own business straight after graduating.

My greatest skills were my artistic abilities, especially as an illustrator, together with my unique ideas and vision to create something different from what was readily available.

You could say that I was very aware of my abilities, had good people skills and always knew what the market wanted and needed. It was this that challenged me to strive to achieve greatness. I never had any fear to fail and never listened to what other people had to say—I was very determined.

The fact that I received such a great response and demand so quickly for my work gave me great confidence and a steady flow of cash, which made it possible for me to continue pursuing my business further.

What was your reasoning behind using your own name as your business name? What do you think are the pros and cons of doing so?

In the beginning I had a strong desire to be recognised as an artist and personality. I knew that the advantage in doing so is that the public feels a connection with the brand and the person behind the brand. As a result I have been able to build a strong profile through my marketing and publicity.

The disadvantage is that sometimes I feel too close to the product and business and take it very personally and emotionally when I receive challenges or feedback that I may not want to hear. Luckily I have a very big following of fans and great respect for my work so it's always been positive to be recognised as the woman behind the brand. I guess you could say that the attachment pushes me to strive for more.

In the early days of your product range, were you approaching retailers directly to stock your products?

Yes, I started off approaching customers myself, and soon after took on sales employees to represent the business and sell the product. When I started exhibiting at trade shows, I was able to attract a greater amount of business from all over Australia. Trade shows were the greatest way for me to expand my business.

Did you have any mentors or business women who you admired to inspire you along your career path?

I have always had many like-minded friends in the industry that pushed and inspired me, and had great support from my family. There have also been many amazing business women in the international arena that I have been inspired by, often in completely different fields of work, namely writers, television personalities and fashion designers.

What has been your biggest challenge in business thus far, and how did you overcome it?

Having sufficient cashflow has always been a challenging aspect of the business as I am continuously growing, expanding, innovating and reinventing myself.

However, I could say that people management was always the greatest challenge in the beginning. Dealing with so many different personalities working in different departments of the company has taught me the importance

*Be patient, be committed, work hard,
plan ahead and be aware that owning
a creative business does not mean
being creative all the time.*

of good leadership, planning, communication and providing staff with a stimulating and creative environment that allows them to grow.

I have always been very sensitive to people's needs and my desire to provide a happy environment and work life balance has helped me ensure a low staff turnover. Furthermore, I have learnt to rely on my intuition when employing the right like-minded people in the business that believe in the product and brand.

Is Cristina Re as it stands now what you initially set out to create as a business? Or did it morph into its current form in a more organic fashion?

I guess you could say that after 15 years in the business, I have achieved what I set out to do—to express my creativity and inspire and delight people through the creation of my many diverse product ranges, from stationery, fashion, home décor, bath and body and food products. I didn't start out to be a stationery designer as such, as I always wanted to see my pattern designs and signature style on many different mediums. Things have evolved and morphed exactly the way I wanted, however it's taken years to do so and a lot of hard work and patience.

How many staff do you have working at Cristina Re now, and what elements of the business do you outsource?

I have about 20 staff members working for me involved in different departments of the business, including design, production, sales, finance, IT, marketing and retail.

I outsource all of my pick/pack and distribution to a third party logistics company that employs people with disabilities. I consider them part of the Cristina Re family.

How hands-on are you in the various aspects of your business day-to-day, such as the retail stores, new product development, acquiring stockists and marketing plans?

I oversee every aspect of the business day-to-day, and am hands on with regards to design and product development. The creative aspect is my passion and I always strive for beauty and perfection in everything I do. I also work very closely with the marketing team to ensure that the business, the brand and my own personal profile is promoted the way I want it.

What advice would you offer designers who want to effectively scale up their business?

To take their time and be patient, be committed, work hard, plan ahead and be aware that owning a creative business does not mean being creative all the time. The creative part is the easy side of things and should come naturally to talented designers—the real challenge is to provide successful management and leadership to inspire and lead people to help grow a company and build the dream.

Where would you love to take your business or yourself creatively in the coming years?

Where do I start? I am a big dreamer and visionary, an overachiever and love challenges, so I see the development of many diverse and unique lifestyle product ranges to expand the Cristina Re offering. I love telling a story in every collection that I release, so I look forward to creating new and unique ranges that set the trends and continue to inspire people.

I love to write and plan to launch a collection of lifestyle and inspirational books that I have been working on for many years, in particular through collaborating with well-known inspirational people in the industry. Furthermore I have plans to work a little more in the television industry with an aim to host my own show and take creativity to another dimension... stay tuned!

*Colleagues and creative people
I've met, worked with and worked for,
have all played a part in forming
not only the architect that I am,
but the person that I am.*

KATE VERNON

Graduate architect

Kate grew up in the country and then went on to
study the B.Sc (Architecture) & B. Architecture double
degree at Sydney University. Kate found leaving home at
age 17 and moving somewhere totally new, where she didn't
know anyone or where she had never even visited before,
to be an overwhelming but totally amazing life experience.
It will always be a time she treasures, not least of all because
of the amazing friendships made, but also because she
sees it as the start of her life in architecture.

After graduating, Kate moved to Melbourne and
was out in the 'real world'. Her first job was with a big
developer, and she hated it. Kate knew that she wanted
to quit after two hours, but it took her two weeks to
actually do it and she has never looked back.

Since then, Kate has worked with some great
Melbourne architects in small, design focused practices
such as Philip Crouch Architects in Sandringham,
Col Bandy Architecture in Albert Park and she is
currently at Basset & Lobaza Architects in Seddon.

The past couple of years have been more about
becoming a new mama to her two gorgeous little
kiddyliwinks, but says this bio isn't long enough to start
rambling on about that, and didn't want anyone reading
to metaphorically start rolling their eyes!

Did you study architecture straight after high school?

Yes. I couldn't wait to take myself off to university and move from the country to the big smoke!

What made you want to go into architecture?

I was lucky because I just knew it was what I wanted to do. I think my mum always having lots of house magazines around at home helped and I used to love drawing up plans of imaginary houses, which are good for a laugh if I look at them now!

Were there many women in your course, or female lecturers?

I think we started first year with a 50/50 male/female ratio, but I think we graduated with more of a 60/40 male/female ratio. I believe the ratio of people working in architecture after 10 years is more like 70 male/30 female.

Where did you work early in your career?

My first job was for a developer, working on big projects. I was so bored and absolutely hated it, so quit after two weeks. The longest two weeks of my life! I then worked for a small architectural practice in Sandringham, working in residential architecture. I love designing houses and working directly with clients. I love working on everything to do with a project and in a small practice, I could get that kind of opportunity and experience.

Is there a lot of learning 'on the job' when you first start as an architect?

I think there's a lot of learning 'on the job' forever as an architect. There's always something new to learn, even simply from the last project and the project before that, which is one of the things I love about it.

How does a client/architect briefing process typically work? What is your favourite part about it, and how can you spot a 'good client'?

The initial brief is really about getting to know the client and finding out what they want out of their project. Clients often have a fairly predictable list of rooms, but designing something for them that delivers more than they could ever have imagined or simply written on a list is so rewarding.

A good client is easy to spot on the first meeting. If a client comes to their project with an open attitude and a genuine trust in the creative process, then I know the project will be a cracker!

How much knowledge about structural engineering, electrical systems, plumbing and other trades do you need to know to keep up-to-date as an architect?

I think you need to have a good understanding of how different consultants and trades work, and where and when they fit in to a project timeline, but it's more about how they work in to achieve the overall design.

Is there much need for professional development in architecture?

It's always interesting and educating to learn about how other architects think, work and manage everything... Their clients, designs, projects, practices and work/life balance.

Is it possible to work solo as an architect, or is it easier in a firm? Which do you prefer?

That depends! I think the perfect balance is working within a practice with other architects so you don't feel isolated, but where you feel like you still have creative control over your jobs and the design.

Did you/do you have a mentor as a young architect?

Hmm. Not officially, but the truth is that lots of colleagues and creative people I've met, worked with and worked for, have all played a part in forming not only the architect I am, but the person I am.

You have two gorgeous young children — did you consider what your career/work life would be like with kids before you had them? How has that view changed?

I don't know if I really thought about it too much before I had my kiddyliwinks, but I've sure thought about it since! I think I always just thought I/we would manage it, but in reality it's not so easy, especially with no family around. But that said, and just in the last few months, it turns out that it has all worked out perfectly. What can I say, good childcare and a flexible attitude from your employer is so, so important.

How has having young children affected your ability to work in your field, in terms of finding work that fits in with a young mum's work/life balance needs?

If you asked me this six months ago, when I first starting thinking about returning to work and looking for a new job, I would have said I was pretty disappointed in some of the attitudes I encountered. I had one recruitment person actually tell me that if I couldn't offer full-time, I didn't have anything worthwhile offering, which really shocked me. I mean, how can that even be true? If someone has 10 years of great experience, that just doesn't make any sense to me. Talk about archaic!

Not one to be deterred, I called a local architectural practice that I always passed and liked the look of, went in, met with them and now work there. I work in an awesome office. Great people, projects and clients, and not least of all is their amazing attitude to work/life balance. They work on a nine day fortnight with an RDO (rostered day off) every second Friday, so know all about having a good life outside of the office, and didn't blink when I said I wanted to work three days a week.

I think there's a lot of learning 'on the job' forever as an architect. There's always something new to learn, even simply from the last project and the project before that, which is one of the things I love about it.

What would you like to see change to offer more balance and flexibility for parents returning to work?

Attitude. Seriously, my new office has the best attitude and I love working there!

Describe an architecture job that you loved for its creativity or the challenges it presented.

I usually end up loving all of my jobs because every one is different. Different people, places and desires, but all of them end up with a unique solution that always seems to work out perfectly for them, despite whatever hiccups arrive. For me, one of the most enjoyable parts of architecture is in the planning and problem solving all of the big and small challenges.

Where do you find inspiration for architectural jobs? What is your process for recording/collating these inspirations?

I guess I come to any new project with my own aesthetic and style, but the site, brief and client are what changes and in turn, what changes each project. What I've learnt from the previous project and project before that also really helps inform my designing.

Have you designed your own home? Or do you wish to?

Our house was already renovated when we bought it, which has been a huge blessing with two small kiddyliwinks (what were we thinking having two kids in under two years?!), but at the same time there are little things that I would have done differently in our house that I just have to accept. Of course, that doesn't stop me constantly re-designing things in my head and on paper!

How would you describe your architectural design style?

Simple, modern, considerate, relaxed... hmm... and bold.

A tutor once said to me that he liked how my designs were handsome, which he then went on to explain as simple, yet bold, so maybe I'll go with that because it's nice and catchy.

Where do you look to for current architecture/design news and inspiration (online/in print)?

Everywhere. Online, design blogs, magazines, other architects, interior designers, artists, cafes, shops, hotels, friends' houses. There's always something great to take away as a design idea from almost anywhere.

What do you think of the current state of Australian architecture? Who is on the cutting edge?

More and more, I'm discovering local architecture that I love. My one grumpy comment about the design publishing industry is that I recognise so many of the same houses published across different magazines. I just think there is so much great local work out there, that it disappoints me when magazines recycle images and stories and I've dropped quite a few subscriptions because of it.

Do you desire to explore any other related (or unrelated!) creative fields?

I would love to work as a florist and have those skills. Any florists out there want to give me a weekend job?

....

*The skills of sewing and patternmaking
are the most important skills to have.
It is not of use to have the most
beautiful piece of fabric if you can't
understand it, design, cut and
construct something from it.*

....

MASAYO YASUKI

Fashion designer

Masayo Yasuki was born in Fukui, on the west coast of Japan. She arrived in Australia as a marketing student and almost immediately upon gaining her business degree, decided that she didn't want to work in formal marketing and instead wanted to pursue her ambitions in fashion and use her marketing skills there. Armed with a second-hand Singer sewing machine, a stack of patternmaking and design books, and fabric usually sourced from op-shops, Masayo started selling her dogstar label at various markets around Brisbane.

Before long a following grew and she moved into a retail business in Fortitude Valley. This soon led to also starting a Brisbane city boutique in the premier street position in Elizabeth Arcade. As the label became more well-known, dogstar expanded its horizons into wholesale, and now stocks over 50 outlets around Australia and New Zealand.

New shops have been opened at South Bank and Paddington and the Brisbane City store has moved to a signature location in Edward Street. The much loved Fortitude Valley store is still kicking along and very much a part of the label's history. After the Brisbane January 2011 floods, dogstar has moved its studio to higher ground at Woolloongabba.

Masayo has two children, who she raises wiht her musician partner at their home on the outskirts of Samford, north-west of Brisbane.

How did dogstar begin? Was it a one-woman show in the early days?

Originally I started at the various Brisbane markets and then in the first shops with a business partner who has since left. From a design aspect, I also worked with a Japanese pattern maker, Akiko, who helped establish the theme and style for dogstar.

What is your process for starting a new collection? Do you begin with a theme or image of the ideal customer?

As seasons change and fabrics for the new ranges become available, I look for the inspiration in things that surround us every day. Nature, buildings and city scapes are the most inspirational. I understand who dogstar customers are, what they want and interpret the collection for them, as best as I can.

dogstar has a very strong visual aesthetic and a timeless style, and doesn't seem to respond to fleeting fashion trends. But do you keep an eye on current catwalk looks at all? Or does your inspiration come from other places and people?

I love fashion and some Japanese and European labels, so I do look at magazines a bit, but take limited inspiration from what others do. The dogstar aesthetic very much derives its existence from structure and silhouette. My customers want to stand out from a design perspective, not from loud colours, brand placement and transient drifts. Day-to-day life is my inspiration, not some fantasy world full of unnatural colours and events.

Your colour palettes are often dark, and fabrics textured and layered. This seems in opposition to Brisbane's sunny and 'tropical' climate! How does living in this environment affect the label's aesthetic?

There is no doubt that darker colours suit the dogstar feel.

Our customers look for the nuance and silhouette that is evident in the richer colours. Yes, Brisbane is a sunny and beautiful city, but not everyone wants to wear a hibiscus shirt.

You have a strong commitment to local manufacturing and using ethically sourced fabrics and materials in your range. Is it difficult to compete with other designer labels who are manufacturing offshore? Do you manufacture any part of the range outside of Australia?

There is no doubt that maintaining that ethic provides a constant challenge and that the industry is highly competitive. It has always been our position to try to make locally. From time to time we have made a very few things offshore, if necessary, but there seems to be unforeseeable and generally unfixable problems when we have. I feel that a lot of control could be lost in overseas manufacture.

There are four dogstar retail stores in Brisbane, but your pieces are stocked through other retailers around Australia. Was it a conscious decision to only have dogstar stores in your home town?

That position really comes from the desire to be in command of the look and feel of dogstar shops. It seems the greater distance, the less control. I am still keen, however, to open up a shop or two down south.

It sounds like you have a very tight-knit team working with you. How do you go about hiring designers, sales assistants and other staff to ensure they fit in with other team members? Do you have a 'must have' checklist?

Enthusiasm and love of our product are my great expectations. If people do not have a passion for what they do, the customer will notice that in any and every aspect of the business.

How hands-on are you in other parts of the business, such as photo shoots, manufacturing, and the retail day-to-day?

dogstar is largely a representation of what I and my design people would surround ourselves in, or about. In all aspects of the business and promotions, we produce and sieve ideas and ultimately it is my job to be the final filter. I try to have as much communication and activity with our customers as I can, and get into the retail stores as often as my schedule dictates.

Sadly, dogstar's studio experienced extensive damage during the Queensland floods in early 2011. What was the initial impact of this? And are you still feeling the effects?

The whole period of the flood and its implications was no fun at all. We have only just finished cleaning up the mess physically and as a business over six months on. dogstar lost a lot of equipment, materials, furniture and bits and pieces. Most of all we lost a great deal of time. Other local designers, business and our staff were incredibly helpful in coming to our assistance with various furniture and production items, storage and even facilities. We cannot thank them enough for their help. The effects of the flood are still with us as a business, but we have moved our studio to higher ground in Woolloongabba which should allow us to enjoy a flood free future.

Did that experience force you to implement systems that would help minimise the effect of unexpected disruptions like 'forces of nature'? What advice would you give to other small business owners about this side of their businesses?

'High and dry' is way better than 'wet and fret'. So always position yourself away from any disaster as much as foreseeably possible. Don't always believe what you are told by landlords and real estate agents. A bit of self-research goes a long way.

What advice could you offer to designers who are just starting out with their fashion labels? Or who perhaps want to take the next step into opening a retail outlet or hiring team members?

There are a lot of people who have a love of fashion. The fashion business, however, has very little to do with parades, parties and glamour. Most of the work is done in planning, experimenting and patterning. The skills of sewing and pattern making are the most important skills to have. It is not of use to have the most beautiful piece of fabrics if you can't understand it, design, cut and construct something from it.

If it is one's dream and desire to design fashion and even open a shop, just be aware that there are many business as well as fashion pitfalls and hurdles along the way. My best tip is always treat your customers and staff with respect, consideration and honesty.

How do you think your own style and aesthetic has evolved over dogstar's lifetime, and are there any new or different directions that you'd like to take the label or your career as a whole?

Fashion is a constantly evolving form. When I started I could not have imagined where dogstar would be today or the styles that we are producing. I love that the business is like driving a souped-up, greasy dodgem car, smashing into everything and thus absorbing the impact. It is this impact and collisions of nature, thought and built environment that allows us to play with design concepts. As to the future, I will continue to ride the dodgems and try to remember to put my helmet on.

What other creative pursuits do you enjoy outside of designing for dogstar?

I love looking after my two children, Naima and Taishi, with my partner River. I love watching them grow and learn.

I enjoy trying to grow my own vegetables. I love to cook, particularly on the weekends when I have a bit more time. It may disappoint that I don't paint, weave or make dream catchers, but sometimes after a long day at dogstar, the remaining extent of creativity I have left is to add a piece of ice to my shot of Patron tequila.

SERENA LINDEMAN

Milliner

Serena Lindeman came to millinery in 1993 in
London following an earlier life as an art teacher.
After training at London College of Fashion she went
to work for Edwina Ibbotson, a well-respected London
milliner. After returning to Australia in 1998 she
established her own business in the Nicholas Building on
Swanston Street in the city of Melbourne.

Millinery continues to be an obsession for Serena.
Her design draws on vintage proportions and
contemporary manipulations of millinery materials.
She teaches millinery and design at Kangan Institute
as well as privately in her work room.

Did you study millinery after school?

Not immediately. I first trained in fine art, majoring in printmaking at Prahran College of Advanced Education, now Swinburne Prahran campus. I went on to become an art teacher teaching two- and three-dimensional design.

When did you first discover you had a passion for millinery?

In about 1992, when I discovered a short course in millinery in the London Borough of Wandsworth. I was teaching in a secondary school and really needed an escape, and millinery just excited me from the first day. I have always loved the creative possibilities in wearing hats, so I was a milliner waiting to happen really.

Did you have a mentor or someone you looked up to when you were starting out in the industry?

That would be Edwina Ibbotson, she was my first employer and one of the fussiest people I know. There were occasional tears when I worked for her, trying to get it right. She stretched me to my limit and to this day I thank her for giving me a standard of workmanship to aspire to. Her work is interesting and constructed to perfection.

What is your process for developing a new design — from idea to finished product?

Stage one is a lot of walking around the table again and again making a mess with all the materials I have in mind. I usually start with the materials and investigate what they will do and how they will behave under my hands. Sometimes it can take ages for the theme to arise for a collection. Eventually the pressure stacks on to the extent that suddenly I am making pieces that begin to please me. Once I get going the hats chase each other out of my mind. Clients are a big part of

I usually start with the materials and investigate what they will do and how they will behave under my hands. Eventually the pressure stacks on to the extent that suddenly I am making pieces that begin to please me. So often once I get going the hats chase each other out of my mind.

my process, sometimes seeing a face and a dress gives me ideas that I would not otherwise have. I see it as a visual conversation with the client and the designer(s) responsible for the garment.

Over the years, do you think your designs have developed a distinct style? How would you describe your style?

I hope they have, I strive for that. I would say my work is about form and volume. I have to remember I am in the fashion industry and that my job is to make women look good.

Do you create a hat yourself from start to finish, or are there parts that you outsource or have assistance with creating?

I'm lucky enough to have an assistant called Connie. She has worked for a number of the milliners around town over the years. She and I work together, each doing the things we do best. She is my right hand.

You hold regular workshops for students at all levels interested in millinery — do you enjoy teaching your craft to others?

I do run workshops, which I really enjoy. A couple of years ago I set up my workroom to take eight seats and I run a number of millinery classes using the space and the equipment we use the rest of the time for making hats for clients.

Where do you turn to for inspiration and new design ideas and to keep abreast of current trends?

I use the Internet to investigate colours and I rely on walking around the city looking at people, into boutiques and looking at fashion magazines (Magnation is a favourite haunt).

What changes have you seen in your industry over the years, and how did you adapt to these changes?

There has been massive change in millinery. Firstly the

hats are now smaller and a lot more interesting than the way they were when I first got back to Melbourne from London. When I got back there was a small number of really talented people working in the industry. Now there are heaps of people (mostly women) turning their hand to millinery. This makes the offering more varied—something for everyone. We have seen a rise in overseas imports as well as online sales of millinery. Nothing stays the same. I Tweet and blog and use Facebook… I need to be able to be found by my clients… Especially if everyone else is doing it.

After so many years running your own business, what is it that still excites you about working in millinery?

I get excited by discovering the new ideas that come up during the season while I am working on my designs. I love the manic aspect of the month before the races, being in demand… I really enjoy taking my stuff to parades and watching the reactions to my work.

What advice would you give to designers who wish to embark on a career in millinery, or similar craft?

You will need to have a second stream of income to survive in this field.

*Art and design is the centre of my life.
I've had a lot of ups and downs in
my career but determination and passion
for what I do is what kept me going.*

GRACE CAMOBRECO

Graphic designer and creative director, Taylor & Grace

A highly creative thinker, Grace is fascinated by the
psychology of branding and human behaviour.
Her belief is that brands need to connect to their
audiences on both an emotional and rational level.
This strategic approach to design places the goals and
objectives of her clients at the forefront of the creative
process — marrying the creative ideas and strategy.

An appreciator of all things creative, it was an
education in fine arts that set Grace on a path leading
to the world of design, where the inventive can become
both practical and artistic. Grace brings this passion to her
work as Principal Art and Creative Director at
Taylor & Grace, always working collaboratively with
her clients to ensure the work meets their needs
and is reflective of their brands and personalities.

Did you develop a passion for art and design from an early age?
The thrill of challenging yourself and creating something beautiful is like nothing else; I get an amazing rush and it puts you on a high that is very addictive. I don't remember a time where my obsession for beautiful things or making beautiful stuff wasn't a part of my life. Growing up in the country in the 80s, art was confined to craft and sewing. It wasn't until high school when a wonderful art teacher encouraged me to start drawing that I really started to feel like I'd found my place.

You studied fine arts before launching a career as a designer — did you do any formal study in design or brand strategy in combination with your fine art studies?
After completing my fine arts degree (I majored in painting and drawing), I stumbled across graphic design. I'd never seen myself as a full time artist. While I loved art and never wanted to do anything else, I always thought I'd become a teacher. But then I found design. I did a diploma in graphic design, and loved every minute of it.

Describe your early career experiences — did you work for other designs studios early on before launching your own studio? What did you learn from these experiences that influenced your own business structure?
Art and design is the centre of my life. I've had a lot of ups and downs in my career but determination and passion for what I do is what kept me going.

My first job straight out of university was an aspiring designer's worst nightmare. I was contracted by a small design and marketing studio to work on a large project — a rubber car hose catalogue. Not only did I typeset the 300 page document but I had to illustrate each and every hose! Surprisingly, I was actually very happy to have a job at all — I knew that finding a first job would be difficult and that studio time and hands-on experience was important. The hose illustration job led to a the offer of a full-time junior design position that provided me with two years of strong creative grounding.

My second job was two years on—I worked as an in-house designer, where I not only created but lived the results of my work. If my creative didn't hit the mark—I was responsible. This was my first real exposure to marketing, business and brand, which taught the value of graphic design and what it means to a business. Design was no longer about me and my own creative expression. It was trial by fire, which has grounded me and made me the pragmatic results-oriented creative head of Taylor & Grace.

Year four I was fired from a role with a design studio after my three month probation. At that stage I was a junior to mid-weight designer, very green, with no real client servicing skills and was hired into a role I didn't have the experience to fulfil.

I was young, immature and naive—my self-worth and sense of identity was wrapped up in my talent and career. This event resulted in a two-year battle with severe anxiety. Strangely enough my anxiety never stopped me from fiercely pursuing my career in design

The lesson in that? My anxiety has largely shaped the designer I am today. The intense desire to 'get it right' has held me in good stead, when I present a first round of concepts to a client 95% of the time a concept is chosen and signed off on the spot. How? I not only take a comprehensive brief, having been in the position of being an in-house designer—I am able to 'walk in their shoes'. I work to ensure an intimate understanding of my client's brand, their business, customers, their market, the required tone and mix this with the aesthetic of the client or brand.

What were some of the challenges you faced in the early days of Taylor &
Grace, and how did you overcome them?

Ah challenges!... Where do I start?

I've been lucky enough to have the perfect business
partnership. Darren Taylor and I have a robust business
relationship and we're the best of friends. As our Managing
Director, Darren has as much drive, motivation and passion
for building and running our business as I do for design.
Many small design agencies don't last the distance because
the overwhelming drive to create beautiful things distracts
them from running a sound and profitable business.

Cashflow for any small business is challenging. We started
Taylor & Grace with enough money to cover equipment and
support ourselves for a short period without taking a wage—
so cash flow right from the start was a constant challenge.

The long hours combined with swift growth and the
resulting stretch and pressure has been one of the biggest
hurdles I've faced over the past five years. Every time I think
I've got a handle on the work volumes, the company grows a
bit more, and there are more resources and skills to find to
manage the increased production. All of this while keeping a
meticulous eye on creative quality control.

Running a creative business is rewarding—managing
a diverse book of clients, the needs of a team of dynamic
creative staff and significant studio workflow is challenging.
We are in a place now where we have a terrific core team
which I can rely on to produce the Taylor & Grace's
exacting standards.

How quickly did the studio grow to engage freelancers and other staff,
and have there been any major shifts in how the studio is structured since
it began?

Our business grew quickly. We began hiring freelancers

from the second year onwards. Back then our studio relied solely on freelancers—writers, marketers, designers and strategists. We've always been very careful not to over-resource. Darren and I are both workaholics and this has worked for us, as we only take on permanent staff if we are certain the forward contracts are there.

Initially Darren and I did everything ourselves. We now have a core team of eight and a stable of consultants and freelancers which number in the 20s.

Do you approach clients with whom you want to work, or do clients come to you via referrals and self-promotion?

Our clients come primarily through word of mouth. Darren has an outstanding ability to build and cement relationships for the business. He has extensive networks which support Taylor & Grace, both commercially and through the pro bono work that we do.

As a studio, what is your approach to pro bono work? Is this built in to your business strategy?

Pro-bono work is something we've always done, because both Darren and I have a background in arts we support several arts organisations. Pro bono for us is about giving back—an important part of creating Taylor & Grace for us was about creating a means to support the people and organisations we care about.

Did you have a mentor or advisor at any point during your career, or when setting up Taylor & Grace?

My mentor in setting up Taylor & Grace was and still is Darren. He's taught me about the ways of business—how to consider and approach business issues as they arise. He challenges me, dishes up tough love when I need it and keeps me honest.

What skills, study or experience would you recommend designers undertake or develop before entering into business for themselves and/or employing staff?

Get at least five or six years under your belt. Without the experience I gained working for others I wouldn't have had the skill, experience or maturity to go out on my own.

If you want less pressure, flexibility to work your own hours or want to focus 100% on building your design skills, don't start your own business.

What advice do you give to people entering the graphic design industry?

» Consider the job requirements and portfolio of the agency you're sending your application to and tailor it accordingly. Your application is one of hundreds—find a way to stand out from the crowd.
» Work on developing a diverse portfolio every chance you get.
» Don't just listen to your own creative voice, learn to listen to your clients—they know their business, audience and industry better that you ever can.
» Do as much work experience as you can—that's how I scored my first gig!

How do you keep your creative ideas fresh and avoid the all-too-common 'burn-out' that can come with running one's own business?

I've never experienced creative burn-out, the creative side of my role is my outlet!

It's what keeps me grounded and sane. Feeding my obsession with new art, design and creative thinking means I constantly and compulsively seek out inspiration all the time, wherever I can find it.

To keep our aesthetic fresh and the creative juices flowing, we fill our studio with inspiration. We are constantly, on a daily basis, reviewing found design and sampling the market. This not only feeds our work but helps us to develop our eye and keeps standards high.

I also try to create a relaxed, fun atmosphere. I actively encourage creative exploration and a positive free-flow of ideas: happy inspired designers create great work.

Decide what you want from that free work (contacts, recommendations, portfolio pieces) and ensure you leverage that work to do what you'd planned.

LOU PARDI

Writer and editor

Lou Pardi grew up in Sydney and moved to Perth
before settling into Melbourne. She is a great advocate
of Melbourne's fantastic lifestyle, culture, people,
coffee, dining and chocolate.

Lou is passionate about sustainability and writes for
Peppermint magazine, an eco fashion and lifestyle magazine
made in Australia, where she previously acted as Melbourne
Editor-at-Large. When not writing about digital media,
sustainability or arts, you'll find Lou photographing her
dinner and posting it to Twitter.

Lou is active in social media and a keen advocate
for the communities which can be built and nurtured
on social media channels.

Tell us about your early career path as a writer.

After high school I went straight into a job as a receptionist in a law firm and worked in admin and as an executive assistant in law firms for about eight years all up. In between law firm jobs I worked in zoos, a pound and in publishing (and yes, the environments of the latter are very similar). I haven't studied journalism although I've always loved writing. I grew up in Sydney, moved to Perth, where I started amateur stand up comedy, moved to Melbourne, did a few comedy festivals, and decided I liked writing more than performing.

How did you build up a portfolio of writing when you were starting out?

When I landed in Melbourne I started writing for *The Groggy Squirrel*, an online comedy site which still exists. It was a fantastic experience because I was learning comedy and getting to interview some of the best comedians in the country. That was where I learnt a lot of my interviewing skills. As a legal secretary I'd done a lot of transcribing so that came in handy in transcribing my interviews.

From *The Groggy Squirrel* I moved on to writing for street press. I started writing for *T-world*, the world's only t-shirt journal (made in Melbourne, distributed internationally) and wrote a lot of the content and edited the magazine, while I still had a day job. There wasn't much sleep happening, but the experience of being involved in every aspect of the editorial was amazing.

Then I met *Peppermint* magazine, and fell in love. I'm still very much building my portfolio, I feel. I've written about arts and entertainment for a long time, food, fashion and sustainability more recently, and social media and digital is my current focus. I feel like I'm on a vertical learning curve. I love it.

When did you start to feel confident with your style of writing, or 'voice' as a writer?

I had a great mentor, Matt Elsbury, when I was doing comedy and I think from working with him—and just the requirement when you're onstage as a stand up you need to be quite present and honest—that came through. I felt more confident using my own voice as a writer after having worked with it onstage for a little while. I've always had the trick that if I feel a bit shy writing, I pretend that I'm writing to my primary school best friend, who's still one of my best friends today.

You were the Melbourne Editor-at-Large of Peppermint magazine... what exactly did your role entail, and how did you initially get involved with Peppermint?

I first saw *Peppermint* at a magazine awards night in Sydney, and the eco/sustainable values aligned really perfectly with mine. I was there because *T-world* was entered for some awards, and *Peppermint* kept winning them! I remember meeting Kelley (*Peppermint* founder/Editor) and Ben (Kelley's husband). They're hardworking, lovely people who really believe in what they're doing, and have given up a lot for it. I pitched a column on palm oil and Kelley kindly published it. I was already really interested in sustainability so it was a natural fit.

My role as Melbourne Editor-at-Large was really just being the face of *Peppermint* locally. Getting out to events and spreading the word. I also acted as a sounding board for the editors (who are based in Brisbane) and initially helped out with some procedural stuff. I've since left the role to concentrate on my new job, but I'm still very close to the magazine and the team.

What are you working on now?

I recently took up the role as Editor of SMK, which is an online knowledge hub covering social media and digital action in the Asia-Pacific. We launch on 1 October 2011 (I'm writing this on 28 August 2011), so right now it's very exciting. We're getting a feel for what our readers are after. They're predominantly client-side marketing, public relations and human resources professionals, so they're after information relevant to them to help them do their job better. It's really fantastic to have a role where you're making excellent content to meet a need, rather than to fill in space between advertisements (which can happen). My role is to guide design of the site, find and brief writers, design procedures, work with the rest of the SMK team on how editorial complements the training programs, edit, post and reach out to our community. Eventually that may involve guiding panel discussions, so I'm looking forward to getting back onstage in a different capacity.

How do you go about getting freelance work? Do you approach publications you want to work with directly with story ideas or pitches?
I have sent pitches in the past, but to be honest I can't remember a time someone who doesn't know me has picked one up. It's not necessarily just who you know, but it does help to be active in social media, engaged with the community you want to write about, and in the right place at the right time. My number one piece of advice to aspiring writers now is find what you love to write about, start a blog about that and build a community. Someone in that community will recommend you. It also helps to go to as many relevant meet-ups as possible.

Doing 'free' or 'for the love of it' jobs are part and parcel of a creative freelancing career. How do you manage those projects with paid work?
I've done a lot of free work over the years, as many writers

and artists have. My current view is that if this is a job, treat even the free work like it is part of a job. Put parameters around how much you will do, how many hours of free work that means per week, and how long you will do it for. Decide what you want from that free work (contacts, recommendations, portfolio pieces) and ensure you leverage that work to do what you'd planned. It's very, very easy to get caught up in delivering free work and not have time to chase or take up paid opportunities.

Decide if you are an artist or a commercial writer. If you are an artist, get a grant. If you are a commercial writer, get some paid work. Also be aware that the more good writers that give away their work for free there are, the harder we are making it for our peers who want to write commercially. We're training industry to devalue good writing. It's a fine balance.

What is your process like for writing gigs — how much time do you spend researching, writing, refining, procrastinating? Is it the same for every job?
I can procrastinate, but often I don't procrastinate as much as I thought I had. I tend to set up pieces by collecting research and images and doing interviews, and then write to deadline (sometimes quite close to deadline). That's not my preferred approach, though. When I'm behaving I use a variation of Pomodoro technique: where you set a timer for 25 minutes, work on one task, then break for five minutes, and repeat – which is great because it keeps me focussed, off social media, and usually I clean my apartment in the five minute breaks.

The time spent preparing and researching varies for each job, but generally my first draft is very close to my final, so there's not a lot of refining. Generally also there's a period of 'marinating' after I've transcribed or finished researching something, where I let my subconscious mull over it until I get an angle or a structure which seems to pop up.

Having a self-employed/freelance career comes with the extra business-related tasks like quoting, invoicing, chasing up payments, and a host of tax related acronyms like BAS and PAYG. How do you handle this side of your day-to-day? What kinds of systems do you have in place?

Quoting is the most difficult part of freelancing for me. It's often hard to know how long a project will take. I have a ballpark hourly rate which I work from, but by and large I'd much rather project cost than provide an hourly rate. I usually invoice when I file the final version of articles, and I have progress payments agreed when I first quote a copywriting project. My invoice says 14 days, but I usually get paid at about 30 days.

I've been very lucky to have most of my clients pay me, but depending what industry you work with, this is sometimes not the case. I usually send an email about 14 days in just asking when they've scheduled my payment for. Projects can blow out by months, so a solo freelance cash flow is a difficult thing to manage.

Constant networking is a big part of any freelancer's world, how do you go about creating new connections and seeking out work opportunities?

Twitter is an amazing resource for both peers and potential clients, leads and building a community. It's a really easy way for people to look you up and see how you interact with your community and what you talk about. Perhaps 10% of my writing is about food and Melbourne lifestyle, but according to Twitter I'm in the know, which is lovely. And very useful if an editor is checking if they want you to write for them.

Going to meet-ups and events around your area of interest is essential, and if you can find a forum or Facebook group to participate in that's useful too. When you see a potential subject or writer you like in the media, add them to your circles in Google+ or drop them a line on Twitter saying you liked what they did. Be nice to everyone.

Would you call yourself a natural networker? What skills do you think help you in this area?

Some people call me a networker and to be honest I find it a little insulting. I know it's not meant that way. I genuinely find people fascinating though, and I spend time getting to know people who I like. Networking for the sake of climbing the ladder is a different game. That's not to say it doesn't work, it's just not for me. My experience has been that if you find good people with similar values to you, you look out for each other, bolster each other up, and are a lot happier in the process.

In terms of skills, good journalists make great networkers. They're genuinely interested in what people have to say and what makes them tick. They're good at considering who they already know who might know someone who can share the kinds of experiences they're writing about. They take notes and follow up if necessary.

You are very passionate about environmental and social issues — can you tell us a bit about the causes you're most dedicated to?

My pet cause in the sustainability area is palm oil. It's a complicated issue which I'm quite conflicted on. On one hand big business is slashing and burning rainforest, destroying ecosystems and murdering and displacing endangered species (orangutans, elephants and tigers to name a few). It's truly awful. On the other hand, the work provided by the plantations supports the economy of the country where it happens, and who are we to say, having cleared so much of our land, that developing nations can't?

My hope is that we can stop the destruction of rainforest, because it is causing animal deaths, and once these animals are extinct, we can't bring them back. Ecosystems are a delicate thing and it's arrogant to think that we can wipe out species and (even putting aside that atrocity) be okay. I'd like to see the workers currently being used to destroy rainforest employed on sustainable oil palm plantations. I'd like to see the orangutans and tiger species which are threatened saved.

Does this play a big part in the freelance writing jobs you take on? Have there been any instances when you had trouble negotiating the need for consistent work and cashflow with adhering to your moral convictions?
Absolutely. There are some jobs I wouldn't take, for example working with an organisation which is an unsustainable palm oil producer. As a foodie, some of the brands I've loved all my life (Tim Tams for example) haven't made the switch to sustainable palm oil and I can't stomach that. I know too many people who have travelled to areas affected by palm oil plantations who have come back with first hand stories about how the animals are suffering there.

On the fashion side, I do work with companies who produce in China (where conditions can be below par for workers and environmental practices), and who use textiles which I wouldn't consider sustainable. The reason I work (very selectively) with those companies is, in some ways, to get behind enemy lines. I don't directly promote them, I probably wouldn't use their products, but I do work with them, and I do get to gain their trust and offer insights about demand for sustainable fashion. I've spent the first part of my sustainability writing experience talking to people who already agree with me. My aim this year, and I imagine for the foreseeable future, is to spend more time with people who disagree with me.

Do you write for fun outside of paid projects? Or do you have other creative pursuits that you enjoy?

While I'm trying not to write for free anymore, I do often take on projects for less money for fun. Writing about Melbourne eating, drinking and experiences is really rewarding, because it's a great city. I don't have any other creative pursuits at the moment, because writing pretty much takes up all of my time.

What projects are you excited about at the moment?

Launching the SMK blog covering digital and social media in the Asia Pacific, more specifically Australia in the short term is really exciting. There's some great stuff happening here which doesn't get covered and there's a readership which needs information which is really great. *The Melbourne Review* is a new print magazine coming soon which will show off our awesome city and *Peppermint* has another great issue coming out soon.

How do you measure success in your own career?

If people let me write for them, I'm thrilled. I feel that an article is a success if it shows an insight into an experience or personality which is unique, and hopefully brings people closer, either because they understand something better, or see their life experience mirrored, which makes them feel less alone. Work/life balance is a huge challenge at the moment, and once I'm sleeping six hours a night (that's the aim) and have a little time to play with I'll be really happy, which is the ultimate career/life aim.

Do you have any advice for aspiring freelance writers and editors?

Begin. Get good at what you do and then value your service. Be kind to each other.

I never had aspirations to be onstage or anything like that, because I was painfully shy. I pretty much had to be forced to play the first Sekiden show.

SEJA VOGEL

Musician and textile artist

Since 1998, Seja Vogel has been an integral member
of Brisbane synth-punk trio Sekiden, who have released
two albums and two EPs. Sekiden's high-energy live
performances have reverberated worldwide, with extensive
touring throughout Australia, Canada, Japan and the US.
2007 saw Seja join iconic genre-mashers Regurgitator as
part of their live touring band, as well as contributing
to their album *Love and Paranoia*, recorded in Brazil.
To date, Seja has travelled with the band throughout
Australia and on numerous overseas jaunts to Japan,
China, Europe and South America. Seja has also lent
her keyboarding and singing skills to touring buddies
such as SPOD and David McCormack.

More recently Seja is performing under her own name.
Seja's solo output is a synthesis of her musical lineage to
date, with future-pop production and blissful
vocal harmonies. She has toured substantially since
the album's release, supporting such acts as
Sarah Blasko, Goldfrapp, and Warpaint.

In between touring and recording, Seja started
successful textile label Pulsewidth for which
she makes little felt replicas of instruments.

You have been involved in the Australian music scene, in bands such as Sekiden and Regurgitator, for more than a decade. Were you very musically inclined growing up?

My parents have always been big music fans so my brother and I were constantly surrounded by it from when we were kids. I took up violin and piano when I was about eight years old and had lessons until high school. But I never had aspirations to be onstage or anything like that, because I was painfully shy. I pretty much had to be forced to play the first Sekiden show.

Last year you released the album, We Have Secrets But Nobody Cares — your first as a solo performer. Having played in bands for so long, what prompted you to go out on your own and release a solo record? Was it something you had wanted to do for a long time?

I think what prompted it was playing in someone else's band for a few years. The time I played in Regurgitator was amazing and I feel so lucky to have been part of it, but it was always their band. So that was one of the reasons I wanted to do something on my own. I also had a lot of down time between tours where I wanted to do something creative, rather than just wasting it, and I had all these ideas and melodies I wanted to work on. So I guess it wasn't something I had wanted to do for a long time, but more circumstantial.

How was the process of promoting yourself as a solo singer-songwriter different to being within a band?

It was very different. In Sekiden I tried to avoid interviews as much as I could, didn't talk on stage, and generally tried to stay behind the scenes as much as I could. I was still learning how to be in front of people and feel confident enough just to play music to others. Then in Regurgitator I was a passenger in a way. Now I really have to think about every little thing in great detail — the music, the instruments, the interviews, the image, the band, etc. It's been a huge learning curve, but ultimately pretty satisfying and exciting that I've been able to do most of it on my own. I have also had help from my record label Rice Is Nice, thankfully, with all the bits I don't know how to do – like get my song played on the radio and things like that, for which I am very grateful.

Are there female singer-songwriters whom you admire or aspire to emulate?

I have always loved the idea of powerful women in music – people who know what they want and how to achieve it, like PJ Harvey and Bjork. They have a vision and don't let others change or compromise it.

The music scene in Brisbane is considerably smaller than in Sydney or Melbourne, and prone to live performance venue closures or fellow musicians moving overseas or interstate. What keeps you in Brisbane, and what do you see as the benefits of a smaller community of creatives?

I really like living in Brisbane. I love that the music scene here is intimate and that we know and support each other. A lot of venues close, but new ones are constantly popping up too. There will always be somewhere to play if you're desperate to, which most of us are. I also like that when you are starting out, there isn't as much competition so it might be a bit of a safer and nurturing environment for shy people who want to make music.

What has been your proudest moment as a musician? Do you have any personal measures of success?

My proudest moment as a musician is a little bit silly. Regurgitator were lucky enough to support DEVO on their last tour of Australia, and Mark Mothersbaugh, who is my absolute hero and one of the main reasons I play and collect analog synthesizers, came up to me while I was sitting out one of the more metal songs in the set and said, "I really like your SH-101" (the synthesizer I was playing). I'm not sure why that was as meaningful to me as it was, but it made me happy for weeks! Also, holding my album for the first time when it arrived was pretty special.

Some people might know you from your miniature felted synthesizer and musical instrument replicas, which have been featured in magazines such as Frankie, and extensively online. How did you come up with this idea?

I used to make little felt things just as presents for friends, but it was never really an idea that I was going to promote or anything. Then, one Christmas I tried to make my friend's entire studio out of felt as a special gift — I made a couple of synths that he had, a little Gibson Firebird, and a little laptop with an open session of Pro Tools and a stereo track on the screen. It took me a really long time but when I had finished it everyone who saw it freaked out and said I should start selling them online. At first I was a little unsure because I was afraid it might take the fun out of it for me to have to make them in bulk. But when I did put them up for sale I loved that so many people were interested.

How long does one felted replica take to make, and were you surprised at how popular they became?

It depends what kind of instrument it is. The synthesizers I make all the time take me about three to five hours, but ones I am not familiar with and haven't made a pattern for can take me up to 10 hours or longer. I made a felt Hammond organ with Leslie speaker and a little stool once that took me about two weeks – its little draw bars went in and out and the Leslie cabinet had a little felt speaker in it. I also made a grand piano with all the strings on the inside and a lid that goes up and down. Those kinds of projects are special though and I wouldn't want to make too many of those or I'd go insane. The little synths or guitars are fun because I can see the progress quite quickly as I make them. I still sometimes find it incredibly amusing that people pay me money to make them tiny felt versions of their instruments.

What other kinds of crafty pursuits do you enjoy? Do you always have a project on the go?

I have always loved crafting, and I mostly have a project on the go. But when things got really busy with my felts I had to give myself a little break between projects. It can get a little stressful to have to sew quickly or to fill orders, so I try to pace myself. But most of the time I just really enjoy it. I sometimes branch out into knitting, or paper crafts, but mostly I just stick to sewing and felt.

Do you have any other musical or creative projects underway that we can look forward to?

I am in the process of writing my second album at the moment. And because I had the felt instruments on my last one, I would love to continue the felt theme and make something really great for the cover of this one. I have many ideas!

....

*When people ask 'who designed that one?',
we can only say 'Polli did', as each design
really is a collaboration. We don't see an
individual ownership in each design.
This philosophy allows us to share our
successes and failures.*

....

TESS LLOYD &
MAJA ROSE

Accessory designers, Polli

With a background in industrial design, the Polli designers
— Maja Rose and Tess Lloyd — have both a creative and
practical skill set. Their products are a fusion of fashion
and product design; industrial and craft processes with each
item hand finished in the Sydney studio. The pair is best
known for their stainless steel jewellery collection. These
light-weight pieces use filigree detail and feature designs
inspired by travel, the natural environment, and their urban
lives. The opportunity to create their own interpretation of
lace is an exciting challenge for the designers.

With all of their products made in Australia, quality
and sustainability are major focuses of this design-based
business. The designers have a strong commitment to
best environmental practice through their production
methods and philosophy that 'good design should never
be disposed of'. They aim to create original, classic
designs that through their durability of materials can
be worn for years and handed down.

The two of you met studying industrial design at university. How soon after graduation did you decide to go into business together?

We worked on many group projects together at uni so we knew we wanted to keep working together in some capacity. Soon after graduating we started working in competing design consultancies and were disappointed we couldn't collaborate, least of all discuss our work anymore. We started designing early Polli products soon after but really only thought of our designs as a hobby and a way of spending time together. At that stage we didn't imagine we would ever have our own business... that took another few years to work out.

After successfully selling your accessories at markets around Sydney, how quickly did Polli develop into a full-time business? Can you tell us a bit about that journey?

As we enjoyed our full-time jobs we really didn't focus on making the transformation from hobby to business for several years. However, wholesale interest grew in our products and we started to take annual leave to exhibit at various trade shows. We realised that one day we'd have to choose. This step was a little daunting as we had always re-invested our revenue back into Polli and had never drawn a wage. We consoled ourselves that it was okay to take part-time jobs if necessary while Polli got off the ground. Luckily for us it was a smooth step and the more time we gave the business the faster it grew. Within a month of leaving our full-time jobs we were on a plane to a New York trade show, within a few more months we had a team of four friends working for us part-time and within a year we purchased our first commercial space.

Does Polli have a company manifesto or philosophy?

Polli has what we term a 'social consciousness' — in that we list our social responsibilities as a brand. These include minimising our footprint and using recycled materials where possible. Polli is recognised as a low CO_2 company and this is something that's really important to us. Manufacturing our products locally in Australia—this can be expensive and limiting but supports local industry. And lastly, creating a supportive work place for young families. Even before the birth of our own children we tried to make a space that was flexible for working mums, many of whom even brought their babies to work with them.

Overall, we believe in lasting design that people connect with rather than wasteful fads.

Have there ever been instances where there has been miscommunication between the two of you about a business or design direction? How did you resolve this?

We're really lucky that we are so compatible and nearly always are on the same page, it's rare that we would ever disagree. We have a very open relationship and are best friends so if something does come up we're quick to chat and resolve it.

How are your roles within the business divided or shared?

We're lucky that we have a lot of overlapping skills so we can support each other but we also have specific roles so that we can specialise and aren't stepping on each other's toes. For example, one might work more closely with suppliers and the other more closely with customers. However, we always work closely on all designs and decision making. When people ask "who designed that one?" we can only say "Polli did", as each design really is a collaboration. We don't see an individual ownership in each design. This philosophy allows us to share our successes and failures.

What is the lifecycle of a piece from initial design concept to finished product? How long does this process usually take?

One of the positive things about manufacturing locally is that the turnaround is generally pretty fast. The process is generally about two months and starts with brainstorming design themes with our team. Then we move to paper sketching our concepts which are scanned (into the computer) and refined in Adobe Illustrator. After reviewing the illustrations we'll get our first samples made, which are tested and refined for production.

Once the final pieces are made we'll hire a model and photographer to shoot the collection and then present it to our wholesale customers at a tradeshow. This process of documenting and selling the collection can add another two months before the collection is actually in store. We'll release two official collections each year and often smaller collections or mid-season releases in between.

Polli has collaborated with a number of artists and organisations. Can you tell us a bit about your favourite collaborations and how these relationships came about?

We've collaborated with different charities and designers in the past but our favourite is definitely our most recent relationship with Melbourne paper cutting artist Emma van Leest. We had been fans of Emma's amazingly intricate hand cut works and seeing a parallel to our own work using positive and negative spaces, we approached Emma about working together. Emma was so enthusiastic we got the ball rolling straight away. We gave her free reign to develop her own design stories and she designed a fantastic series based on early explorers like Captain Cook and the ventures the Endeavour took to exotic new lands, to discover things like tropical pineapples and royal dodo! We then met face-to-face with Emma to transform these intricate collages of imagery from detailed paper cuts into miniature jewellery pieces.

Environmentally friendly business practices are extremely important to you both, and all Polli products are manufactured in Australia. Have there been times where a product design you loved could not be manufactured because it wasn't able to be produced cost-effectively in an environmentally friendly way in Australia? Or do you always consider the environmental production and cost limitations before embarking on the design phase?

As manufacturing in Australia is part of our company ethos we often consider our manufacturing options before embarking on a new product range. It does mean some processes are too expensive to do locally—making affordable products is also important to us. When we initially started Polli as a hobby, our goals were to make something we would use ourselves, something we could afford, something with a fast turnaround (impatient ladies) and something we could have fun doing together. So high end labour intensive products just aren't Polli!

We do consult with our manufacturers to see what other processes they use that might be suitable for a Polli product, this way we don't get disappointed with designing something that can't be made in Australia within the right price range.

You wholesale to many stockists around Australia and internationally —have you the desire to open a flagship store? Is it something you have considered?

We've talked about it and while it's tempting we feel our products are physically too small for their own store. We'd end up selling a lot of other products but we feel this would distract us from our own brand. Our retailers do an amazing job of selecting different products that complement each other each season.

Do you have a business mentor or advisors that you turn to when strategising for your business?

Over the years we've met many impressive women who
are inspiring to us in what we do, one of whom is Shelley
Simpson, the founder of Mud Australia. Shelley has built
her brand from a small one-woman cottage industry into
an international brand. We've travelled with Shelley to
interstate and international trade shows and we're lucky
she's a great listener and always willing to offer advice.

*Polli has exhibited at a number of large trade shows in Australia and
overseas. Do you have any tips for small businesses about to embark
down the trade show path?*

Trade shows can really make or break you—financially
and emotionally. If you can, try to visit the show as a guest
to establish if it's right for your product. Consider the
other brands showing and perhaps survey your wholesale
customers to see if it's an event that they buy from. If it's an
international trade show, investigate if you're entitled to
any financial export assistance and consider working several
goals into each trip to ensure that you're making the most of
your time and finances. In either market it's important to
consider pricing to make sure that you understand wholesale
terms and margins.

Trade shows are a great opportunity to meet the buyers
and make a great impression. We always have a little
sweet for them to take away, in the United States we have
Caramello Koalas, which go down a treat. The worst thing
you can do is be grumpy if the show is not going well. You
never know who is around the corner to put in an order.

*You have a small team who work with you in your office, and also have
satellite team members around Australia and overseas. Can you explain
a little about their roles at Polli?*

We have a great team and with less than 10 people we
have enough man (or woman) power to get things done,

but we're at a comfortable size for us to manage without distracting us from what we do. The team specialises in their different roles; satellite members work in areas like sales, marketing, web development and public relations while our in house team work in areas like design, management, customer relations, production and fulfillment.

Describe an average day in the Polli office.

Each day at Polli starts and ends with a cup of tea. We're a small all-female team and with lots of young kids in the mix. We all keep slightly different hours and days. Often someone will ride their push bike. The space is very open plan so we'll share music and talk openly with each other. Each day we stop for an organic, vegetarian communal lunch which gives us time to catch up and nourish ourselves without waste or food envy! Everyone is very hands-on, and depending on the day we might be asking for feedback on new designs, making samples together or discussing ways we can improve our web store.

While we all have our specific tasks there are many things we brainstorm together, like props and models for the next shoot, newsletters for our web and retail customers or what we'll post on the blog each day.

You have built Polli as a business that is supportive of women who work and have young families — what kind of systems do you have in place to ensure flexibility and efficiency in your workplace?

To provide a supportive working space for young families, we offer flexible working hours. While it sounds simple, paying everyone by the hour allows people to come and go as they please, especially if they need to drop off/pick up their children. We have also had several 'Polli babies' in the studio over the years (long before we had our own) so we've always had a lot of toys to play with. More recently this has grown to include a cot, change table and purpose built play area. Where possible we also allow work to be taken home to be completed during nap times.

What creative things do each of you enjoy doing outside of Polli?

Maja is an amazing knitter and crocheter. She's part of a secret knitting society called Ravelry, which is sort of the Facebook for knitters. She can tackle any pattern and makes beautiful handmade clothes. We've also done several courses together like silversmithing (we got separated for talking) and sewing, which a lovely pattern making friend taught us. It's been lovely being able to make clothes for different little people we know.

PIP LINCOLNE

Author and retailer

Pip Lincolne was raised in Tasmania on a steady
supply of handmade things and homemade cakes.
She now lives in Melbourne with her family, cooking
nice dinners and making a crafty living through
her blog and shop Meet Me at Mike's.

Pip is the author of three craft books: *Meet Me at Mike's*,
Sew La Tea Do and *Make Hey! While The Sun Shines*.
She is craft columnist for *Frankie* magazine and makes
regular appearances on radio and television
to encourage people to make things.

Some may be familiar with Meet Me at Mike's story, but can you recount for us how it all began?

Way back, in the olden days, when Melbourne was not quite so delightfully laden with craft markets and crafty shops, we ran a skate franchise in Richmond. We sold skateboards and limited edition tees and figurines and other cute stuff. We were a bit guy-craft, I guess. I was not much into guy-craft, being a girl and all. I decided it would be a great idea to make the shop over into something more girly and Pip. We were not trading very well, doing the guy-style thing. So change it I did. This was back in 2005–2006.

I decided that selling the things I loved would be the most meaningful, least hard-sell option. So I began filling the shop with vintage, handmade and cute. My partner thought I was mad, a lot of people thought I was mad, really. I dragged my sewing machine out onto the shop counter and refashioned vintage dresses in-store. I scoured op-shops for cute knick knacks. And I invited local makers to put small runs of their work in-store too.

I started a blog, I started running 'Stitching Nights' in-store, providing embroidery tuition, cupcakes and champagne for groups of cute gals. Before I knew it, *Frankie* came knocking wanting to profile us! Hot diggity!

The 'bricks and mortar' retail environment has changed dramatically in recent years. What do you see as the future for independent retailers? What would you like to see happen?

Well. Um. It's not for the faint hearted. And I am quite stellar in the bravery department, but the economic climate and figures over the last 18 months have been the proof of the pudding for me. The pressure has gotten a bit too squeezy and we have decided to close the shop front in favor of other projects and an online incarnation of Meet Me at Mike's.

I think if you are a sensitive, creative type, you can take these kind of knocks a bit harder than most. So after 25 years in retail we are retreating for a while. I wouldn't rule out a shop again down the track, but at the moment we are juggling too many things, and we need all those things to be working out great. The shop has just become too much work for little financial reward. As much as we have loved it, LOVE DON'T PAY THE RENT!

I feel a bit worried for independent retailers. I think that online shopping is so convenient and completely seductive in the wee hours with a glass of wine. People are definitely spending a lot of money online, money they would once have spent in shops like ours. And also the bricks and mortar stores are serving as showrooms for brands and designers/crafters. People can visit and check out products, but will then very often go home and buy the same item they just looked at in-store online (perhaps justifying it in terms of lower price point). That makes things very hard for shops!

Rents are also way too high for niche retail. I would really love to see some subsidised retail spaces, supported by state or local governments (or even federal!). I think it would be great if some of those fledgling retailers (or even old hands like us!) got a bit of support and a foot in the door. We're battling a global marketplace and big business, as well as inflated rentals and huge overheads. It would be lovely to get a bit of a helping hand, especially for businesses who really contribute to the cultural tapestry of a city.

Opening a shop is the dream of a lot of independent makers and design enthusiasts... Having been in the retail industry for so long, what advice would you offer a new shopkeeper?

Well, here is what I would say:

» Make it your own! We have had a huge amount of people come through our doors over the years, delighting at what we are doing and vowing to open a shop doing the same thing. Make sure there is ROOM for your business in your city or town. Don't just replicate what someone else is doing, but rather put your very own stamp on things. Make your shop a unique reflection of you and what you love.

» Make sure you have PLENTY of money in the bank! The killer thing about retail is that there is no consistency whatsoever. You need a good buffer to tide you over and see you through the tough times, because lean times are inevitable.

» Be compliant! Please make sure that you keep accurate records, pay your GST, file your bank statements and keep your house in order, in general.

» Don't work seven days! Make sure that you give yourself time to rest and recover each week, because self-employment can be all consuming. Take some time for you!

» Have an exit strategy! As excited as you are about your business today, some day down the track you might want to move on. Plan for that. Think about how you might bow out, if you need to. And also think about how long you are willing to stick it out if it's not working. One experienced retailer I know has a '12 month rule'. If a new shop is not making money at the 12 month mark she will shut it down.

» Be social! It's a must to have a blog, Twitter and Facebook account for your business.

And what advice would you offer to makers who want to sell their work in a retail environment?

I think this is a tougher call than people think. You really need to think about this early on in the game, especially when you are pricing your work. I know a lot of crafters who are selling their work at a WHOLESALE price on sites like Etsy. Make sure you think ahead and sell your work for the desired RETAIL price on Etsy. This way you get a bigger margin on the things you sell yourself via Etsy, and any future retailer can sell your work for the exact same price. Don't sell yourself short!

I think if you are approaching retailers, it's a good idea to have a good web presence as well as a quality product. Retailers are busy bees, so if they can view your work online in the dead of night after they've finally shut up shop, you stand a better chance of being stocked. Having your work featured on blogs and magazines is also a good way to catch a retailer's eye, so make sure you promote yourself well and make yourself known. Markets are also a great way to be seen by shopkeepers (just make sure you have your wholesale/retail pricing situation sorted, because no retailer will stock your product if you are selling it for half the price at your local craft market!).

You have just released Make Hey! While the Sun Shines, your third book. Tell us how your relationship with your publisher Hardie Grant began. Did you approach them with the initial idea for a book of craft projects?
When we started Meet Me at Mike's there were a lot of American craft books being published, but there was no book detailing the Australian contemporary craft scene. I knew Hardie Grant as a foodie/cook book publisher, and I figured that a craft book was just like a DIY recipe book! So, I went to their website and emailed them my idea. I didn't even write a proposal, I just wrote a short email. Lucky for me, a few of the Hardie Grant publishers and management shopped at Mike's and knew all about what we were up to (I did not realise this!). Within a couple of weeks I had a

meeting with Mary Small (my publisher for *Mike's*) and we were away! I think I was VERY LUCKY and my timing was perfect, to be honest!

What surprised you about the processes involved with putting together the book Meet Me at Mikes? And what did you learn that helped you write Sew La Tea Do and Make Hey?

It was a very LONG process! It took about two years, due to all kinds of issues getting in the way (including change of release dates for the book). I was also really surprised at how hard it was to coordinate the book and deal with so many creative people. We profiled 24 other crafters in *Meet Me at Mike's*, each with their own eccentricities! It was quite a challenge to keep everyone feeling positive about the project at times, because I think creative people are very conscious about how their work (and their lives) might be represented. I think also because a lot of those crafters did not know me personally, they were unsure of the tone/final aesthetic of the book. Luckily they were all very happy when they saw the end result, but I totally had to earn my stripes with some of them, which was unnerving! All that aside, I feel really lucky to have worked with so many talented ladies. The book would have been nothing without them!

I really love the process of piecing a book together, and working on the first book showed me that not only was I good at it, but I was probably better off showcasing my own work in future books… Far less opportunity for crafty conflict! Apart from that, I really wanted to challenge myself, coming up with 25 projects of my own and ensuring they would be the kind of things people would want to make!

Once I knew the process, I was able to become more involved in the design of the book, which has been really interesting and rewarding. I love working on photo shoots.

*Don't just replicate what someone else
is doing, but rather put your very own
stamp on things. Make your shop a unique
reflection of you and what you love.*

I love styling. I love cobbling all kinds of things together into one cohesive volume. And most of all, I love encouraging people to dip their toes in the craft water!

You're a contributor to popular websites like Michi Girl and magazines like Frankie. Have you always enjoyed writing, and does it come easily to you? What has made you want to pursue this side of your career in recent years?

I have always wanted to be a writer, and I have always written stuff. When I was about 12 I used to send poems in to *Dolly* magazine, hoping they would be published (two were!) or that (Editor) Mia Freedman would snap me up as their youngest ever features writer! OMG! Writing does come very easily to me, because I write the way I talk. I don't labour over it, but rather just blab away in my own voice and something fairly passable usually surfaces!

Because writing for magazines and writing books has been a lifelong dream, I made sure that I really did not let go of it, rather that I kept chipping away and putting myself out there and taking risks in a writerly fashion. I was lucky enough to be approached by Jo Walker from *Frankie* for their craft pages and have been writing for them for the last couple of years.

I really feel that writing is a big part of who I am, and I really want to improve and develop that part of my life. I really want to write professionally for the rest of my days!

You blog prolifically and are very active in the social media world — how much time do you dedicate to your blogging each week? Do you plan blog posts in advance or do you write them on the fly?

I spend a couple of hours a day (if you cobble together all those 10 minute snippets) combined on blogging, blog reading, other professional development reading and social media. I really love it, because it is a big part of my job! I love being part of a wider online community and seeing what everyone is up to. I also really like sharing tips and skills and ideas and experiences via my own blog. The other good thing about this online world is that we are all like a bit of a cheer squad for each other. It's really easy to seek out supportive or super positive people to buoy my mood and keep me motivated.

I never plan blog posts. I am completely undisciplined in that regard. I like to be spontaneous and to have a bit of a stream-of-consciousness thing going on. I think that one of the great things about blogging is the immediacy and currency of posting. Sometimes I think that too much planning would make my blog stale or too magazine-y... I much prefer to just belt something out (which may take anything from two minutes to two hours to compose or write) and hit publish! I think there is a freshness and a real honesty in that which can't be beaten, for me at least! It is totally of the time.

Have you experienced any negativity from having such a high profile in the online world? How do you deal with those situations?
The media has dubbed me 'The Queen Of Craft' so of course I have had some nasty comments and a bit of hate mail due to my coronation! I think it's to be expected. I don't think it's to be excused though! It's a weird quirk of human nature to observe and idealise the lives of others, feel inadequate and then feel the need to attack or critique. I have learned to just breathe through those kinds of nasty jibes and put my fingers in my ears. I am not saying I don't find it hurtful, but I think that it's important not to feel victimised by that kind of stuff. Often people think that they know all about you, and they base their assumptions or snark on their own personal perception. I like to think that

if they actually knew me, they would fall completely in love with me and never troll me again. LOL.

The nature of the Internet means that a bit of anonymous nastiness is inevitable, unfortunately. I will never forget when I posted about my dog getting run over and someone posted an anonymous comment saying "Maybe it's karma". I mean, SHEESH!

I really think we need to unlearn this culture of competition and criticism. I think we should look at each other's achievements and offer our congratulations. I think that we can all keep this boat afloat and sailing beautifully if we just take the time to celebrate each other. I am not sure that Anonymous thinks that, though…!

How do you see the world of creative blogs evolving in the future? What are you starting to see happen?

Oh blogging, especially creative blogging, has just exploded hasn't it?! It's like some kind of yarny, inky, fabricky kaboom! I think it is WONDERFUL. I think that people blogging regularly about their creative lives can only lead to very good things. I am a firm believer in documenting our lives as a tool towards positivity and personal growth, and blogging is a super simple way to do that.

I really like that people are using all kinds of platforms to share or express their creative lives. And I'm also loving the way that social media platforms like Twitter and Facebook offer a further layer of connectedness for the creative community.

I think we are all learning a lot from each other, not just in terms of craft skills, but also in terms of technology, photography and online skills too. I've really noticed a lot of newish blogs popping up, with a focus on great content, beautiful photos and great blog design. I think that's so ace.

The bar is being raised all the time and we are challenging ourselves to do a better job every day. I think that's so positive and inspiring.

I am liking less the big push toward blogging for fame or fortune. I think that if you start out with those kinds of goals things can get a bit ugly. Blog from the heart, I say.

The annual Softies for Mirabel appeal and the Brown Owls craft groups are two initiatives that you started, and both really bring the local craft community together. What do you enjoy most about devising projects like these?

I have quite a healthy readership, which can be unnerving at times. I decided that one of the ways to feel a bit less narcissistic was to use that readership to do some good stuff and to connect people in crafty and friendly ways. So that is what I did. Apart from Brown Owls (our crafty club) and Softies for Mirabel (our annual toy drive to benefit The Mirabel Foundation), we have run lots of community arts projects via our shop window, we've collected donations of household items and new heirlooms for those affected by Black Saturday, we've collected books for a local school who were a bit short and we've done some work with the Fitzroy Learning Network (in return for use of their hall, too!). It is really important not to professionalise and commodify ourselves too much, I think. We need to be really careful that we are doing things to contribute to the community too, even in our creative lives. Happiness and success is not just about the bottom line, it's about finding ways to be a positive, active part of this big village we all live in.

Who do you admire in the creative business world?

Jo Walker, Louise Bannister and Lara Burke from *Frankie* Magazine: Together they have grown a teensy mag into the much loved must-buy that it is now. They've done it with lots of hard work, a clear vision and a real passion for what they do. I love that. I love how different *Frankie* is from the other magazines, and how they have stayed true to themselves. And I super love that it is a vehicle for creatives of all kinds, some of whom may go unnoticed without a bit of spruiking from Team Frankie.

I'm also a mega fan of Beci Orpin, book designer Michelle Mackintosh, Dawn Tan, my studio buddy Victoria Mason, Outre Gallery curator and artist Gemma Jones, Abi Crompton from Third Drawer Down, Geneine Honey from Little Salon, Cathy Hope, Chanie Stock, Emma Greenwood, Ghostpatrol and Miso, Ink and Spindle, Catrabbit and a whole host of others. I think I would need 12 pages to include everyone!

Are there particular challenges to running your own business that you think are associated to being a woman?

I have three kids, and I really do struggle with the work/life balance thing. I think this is a big part of us streamlining our life and moving the shop online. It's just really so hard to be doing everything in ways that are good enough, let alone great. Things fall through the cracks sometimes and that can be stressful.

I am really lucky, because we have always structured our life so that we can get our kids to school and pick them up afterwards. We don't need to use childcare or aftercare, so that has been great. But the flip side of that is that when they are at school we are really running like the clappers to get stuff done, and it feels quite chaotic at times. Of course these are issues that dads have too, but I guess I am the kind of gal who is wracked with feelings of responsibility and 'mother guilt'. I really do give myself a hard time, sometimes!

What is the biggest misconception that admirers of your work might assume about you?

That we make a lot of money. My partner and I have both worked multiple jobs to keep the doors of Meet Me At Mike's open over the last few years! Maybe we should have applied for an arts grant... ?! Oh well!

Tess McCabe is a creative all-rounder. After completing a Bachelor of Design Studies, Tess cut her graphic design teeth in publishing and book design and travelled extensively before launching her solo graphic design practice in Melbourne in 2008. Craving connection with her creative peers, in 2009 she took the reins of Creative Women's Circle (CWC), a national community for women working in creative industries. In 2015 she reformatted CWC into a not-for-profit association and held the position of President on its board for three years. Creative Minds is her independent publishing company and passion project, creating books and resources that assist creative professionals and inspire them to think big about small business.

Tess enjoys learning from and promoting the work of other creatives whom she admires. Her passion for seeking out ways to work smarter, not harder, has become acute as she maintains her businesses alongside the needs of her young family. When not 'at work', you'll find her painting, weaving, podcasting, reading or devising grand plans, most often with a strong cup of tea in hand.

ALSO FROM CREATIVE MINDS

Owning It: A Creative's Guide to Copyright, Contracts and The Law by Sharon Givoni

The Leap Stories: Intimate Interviews on Overcoming Fear, Choosing Courage Over Comfort, and Designing a Fulfilling Career by Kylie Lewis

creativemindshq.com
@creativemindshq